D0358820

Two Generations of Soviet Man

Two Generations of Soviet Man

A Study in the Psychology of Communism

By

JOHN KOSA

Chapel Hill

THE UNIVERSITY OF NORTH CAROLINA PRESS

Manufactured in the United States of America

PRINTED BY THE SEEMAN PRINTERY, DURHAM, N. C.

TO MY WIFE

memores operis fidei vestrae et
laboris et caritatis et sustinentiae spei

I Thess. 1: 3

ACKNOWLEDGMENTS

THE IRON CURTAIN was tightly rolled down and the Communist world was practically inaccessible to Western scholars when I began collecting data for this study. From the very beginning of my work, however, I had the assistance of many friends who generously furnished me with otherwise unavailable information and comments. In particular, I wish to express my gratitude to scholars and writers of Hungarian origin, to Imre Bernolak, Stephen Borsody, István Csicsery Rónay, William Juhasz, Mrs. Judith Le Bovit, August J. Molnar, Julius Rezler, and Francis S. Wagner in America and to John S. Eros, Paul Tabori, and Stephen Ullmann in England. Imre Székely Molnár and L. L. Telekes in Canada were extremely helpful in arranging interviews with Hungarian refugees. My old friend, Robert Major, put to my disposal not only his vast knowledge but also his rich collection of pertinent material.

For many details on the satellite countries I am indebted to such authorities as Jiri Kolaja, Mrs. Sheila Patterson, Joseph S. Roucek, and Irwin T. Sanders.

My particular thanks are due friends and colleagues in Ithaca and Chapel Hill. Long discussions with Mrs. Rose K. Goldsen, Gordon F. Streib, and Wayne E. Thompson fruitfully contributed to the formation of the ideas presented here. In many other phases of the work I received encouragement and assistance from Robin M. Williams, Jr., Robert E. Coker, Jr., Robert C. Elston, and Bernard G. Greenberg.

I owe gratitude to the readers of the manuscript whose comments helped to clarify many points and passages, to

Mrs. R. S. Arnold, Mrs. Frances Adkins Hall, Mrs. Baxter K. Hathaway, Mrs. Beatrice M. Vicroy, Arthur Candib, and Richard L. Means.

My final word of indebtedness should go to the University of North Carolina Press for its continued interest in the work and the many helpful suggestions offered.

JOHN KOSA

CONTENTS

Two Generations of Soviet Man

I. INTRODUCTION

Most books arise from a personal relationship between an author and a topic. Writers work under the spur of a motivation. If they were not personally involved in one or another point of their chosen subject, few of them would persevere in the labor of clarifying ideas and putting them into words. The principle of scientific objectivity, so dear to academic writers, is not incompatible with this relationship. It requires, however, that the author should strive to overcome his personal involvement and write as an unprejudiced observer. The historian, political scientist, psychologist, or sociologist endeavors to achieve this objective in his own way and must be judged by the degree of impartiality he has shown.

The present book attempts to interpret a psychological aspect of Communism, a subject that all too often evokes the free outburst of human emotions. It is therefore only fair that the author should state what the extent of his personal involvement is and what efforts he made to overcome subjective judgment. This statement is needed not as a personal clarification but rather as a summary of the problems that will be investigated here.

My first relationship to this topic was nothing else but the idle curiosity of my youth. I grew up in Hungary in the 1930's, the decade of the depression, under a government far removed from the ideals of democracy and social justice. Communism was an illegal movement, and anybody arrested as a Communist was sent to the military prison and even to the gallows. Yet, there were some illegal party members and even more sympathizers. They hid their convictions, but one could feel their presence in those small circles where students, young teachers, and writers gathered. As we listened to an animated speaker, holding the attention of the group in the heated atmosphere of our nightly debates, when we, as young men, talked over all the issues of the time, his accidental phrase, unexpected intonation, or blush of the cheek suddenly set our minds into motion: "Is he an *illegal?*" We never asked the question openly, because this might have benefited the political police, hated and feared by all of us equally. Having no sure answers, our minds nevertheless worked and reached their own conclusions. Youth is not suspicious by nature, but this was a national guessing game in which everybody participated according to his convictions, temperament, and interests. I, being a student of psychology, played it according to my rules and wondered not about the special case of this or that acquaintance but rather about more general problems: What makes a person a Communist and what moves him to take the heavy risks he faces if he is detected? What rewards does he hope for or what drives of self-destruction does he follow?

There were no good answers, and our guessing game remained a crude play. When in 1945 the party came out in the open and our guesses could be verified, many of those whom we had thought to be party members turned out to be nonmembers, and many of those whom we had never suspected appeared to belong to the inner circles of Communism. There was, however, no chance to reanalyze the apparent failure of our judgment, since by that time our lives became deeply involved with another aspect of Communism—a less idle and more painful involvement than the first one. It was a matter of self-assertion, a crucial matter of manhood.

In 1945, as the war ended and the old regime collapsed, the Communist party emerged as a major governing party of the country. It came at the heels of the Russian army that was routing the Germans, and a German defeat has always been heartening to the independent-minded Hungarians; it promised peace after the ravages of war and social justice after an era of injustice and oppression. It was received accordingly. A few people greeted it with enthusiasm, many with a cautiously advanced confidence, many others with a neutral "wait-and-see" attitude, and a few, again, with hostility. We, the intellectuals of democratic persuasion, were likely to be at the middle of this line, somewhere between cautious confidence and "wait-and-see," but could not stay there for long. As the party began to make itself heard through its spokesmen and press, it expressed a philosophy that made us first uneasy and then militantly opposed.

Our first impression was that the party, with the repetitiousness of a stubborn child, claimed to know everything better than anybody else, claimed always to be right and asserted that the citizen can be right only to the extent of his agreement with the party. Soon we had to realize that this was more than a pose of self-aggrandizement; the party as a political power wanted to accomplish much more than a poseur or a braggart wants. It wanted to change us, the sundry citizens of the country, to transform us into images of its liking; it wanted to rebuild our inner selves in the way that an old piece of furniture is rebuilt. For us, who regarded our personal convictions as inviolable, this program slowly grew into a personal threat; we tried to fight and resist it, but our resistance was whittled away in thousands of ingeniously devised ways. As it became more and more difficult to maintain the sanctity of our own selves, the dilemma before us was clearly posed: one had either to conform to the program of the party or renounce his minimal requirements of personal security, material welfare, and happiness.

Facing this dilemma, many of the intellectuals decided to leave their native country. A decision of such importance was made from many motives, but one of the motives was foremost in our minds: we calculated that the opportunity of living according to our liking was worth the risks of escape and immigration.

That night in January, 1949, when stealthily I walked across the muddy fields of the international border and reached the Western occupation zone of Austria marked the end of my personal relationship with Communism. With some delay, the walk led me to America. For the coming years, amidst the labor of creating a new existence, amidst the well-tempered amenities of academe, Communism receded from my mind. The great human ability to forget and then to revive old memories is the sound basis of our psychological growth. In my case, it was long research in some other field that eventually revived the curiosity of my youth and broadened the youthful questions into more general forms.

We usually take it for granted that the citizen pledges his allegiance to the "right" cause but withdraws it from the "wrong" one. Hence, the usual subject of our inquiries about commitment to cause is: "How can we discern the right from the wrong?" We usually carry out such inquiries in terms of moral philosophy. Yet at the same time a purely psychological inquiry about these matters is necessary: "What makes a man pledge his allegiance to a cause of any kind?" Similarly, we are wont to take it for granted that any person adapts himself to his social environment, and scholars investigate this problem: "What kind of socialization process will produce the most perfectly adjusted citizens?" Yet it is again necessary to investigate how malleable human nature is in its adaptation to any environment and how successful a powerful organization can be in reshaping the inner selves of people.

By the time the youthful questions presented themselves in such general forms, I felt that time had removed the personal impact of my experiences and I could approach the old topic with objectivity. As I began to work with the source material, the pieces of information seemed to fall into their proper places and the answers to the questions that had evaded me for a long time emerged as the obvious, natural explanations. The result of these investigations is the present study.

The founders of psychology, Sigmund Freud and William James, could draw on their personal experiences and present them as the general rules of human behavior. A scholar less skilled in this kind of subjective examination may find some grave dangers hidden in that approach. For him, it is safer to rely on the objective sources of knowledge and to present those sources in accordance with the accepted rules of research methodology. The objective method of data collection, however, is still a pious wish in the Soviet countries, because there it is still impossible to interview a representative sample of the citizens, to survey public opinion, and to administer certain types of personality tests. Thus, the present study had to use other sources of data from various fields. It took Hungary as the central point of its investigation, but attempted to offer evidence from other countries also to suggest that its theses are not specific to one country but general to Communism.

Printed texts are the best sources concerning the teaching and practice of the Communist superego—as the main psychological aspect of the movement will be called in the following pages. To be sure, the writings of the party theoreticians, the speeches of the political leaders, the reports of the newspapers are all too often ritual texts, redundant with commonplaces and devoid of sincere or factual information. Their perusal frequently proves a frustrating experience for the research worker. The text of a Soviet constitution or law may give some clues to the psychology of the Com munist creed; some official speeches of great political importance are of no use at all; while a short or half-hidden phrase of a news item may contain much revealing material.[1] But any psychologist who attempts to analyze the personality of an individual is likely to have the same experience: he must wade through much "useless" material before he finds the revealing traits and meaningful patterns.

The party is loquacious, and there is no dearth of material expressing its official words and attitudes. But the Communist press turns reticent when it comes to the spontaneous ideas and deeds of the citizens, and particularly so if those spontaneous ideas are contrary to the will of the party. When looking for the testimony of citizens, I discovered, somewhat to my own amazement, the poets. Poetry is the eternal device for expressing sincere feelings, and no state censorship or thought control can entirely stifle it. The poet, of course, is not the typical representative of society at large but is a person with exceptional ability in sublimating everyday experiences. The Communist poets could get printed many thoughts that the average citizen had no chance to voice; as a consequence, their ideas will be repeatedly quoted here.

The opinions and attitudes of the average Soviet citizen can be ascertained in difficult, roundabout ways only. Since refugees from Communist countries are accessible to Western scholars, quite a few attempts were made to gauge the political attitudes of Soviet citizens through the testimony given by refugees. At one point this procedure usefully contributed to our meager knowledge of the Soviet world, but soon it turned out to be a rather unreliable, even misleading, source of information. After all, refugees are a biased sample of the population. They are people who have rejected the Soviet system (or perhaps the fatherland), have chosen to leave their native land, and have renounced those strong ties that everybody feels toward his childhood environment; their backgrounds, feelings, and opinions are not characteristic of those people who stayed at home.[2] In addition, the more time an immigrant spends in America, the less representative he becomes; the more frequently a refugee contacts the anti-Communist political organization of the West, the more his bias is enforced. As a result, the average refugee in his overt statements is likely to give us reinforced stereotypes, or what he *thinks* the public opinion in the West expects to hear from him.[3]

For lack of better sources, I planned to employ the testimony of refugees in this study, but in the "original," nonrationalized form that might indicate covert opinions and attitudes. I resorted, therefore, to the method of "tell-a-story," used in the same fashion as a projective technique in psychology. A small, selected group of Hungarian refugees were asked to tell that fictional story which, in their opinion, best characterized the Soviet system. This procedure assumed that the fictional character of the story would free the informants from those controls which operate whenever "ego" and "truth" are involved and that the stories would reveal attitudes in their uncensored forms.

Thirty-one males from the well-educated classes of Hungary who had left their native country after the revolution of 1956 were selected as informants. They were selected because a considerable amount of "objective" information was available on each of them. This information, furnished by reliable persons of Hungarian background and long American residence, gave a certain insight into the character and veracity of the respondents.

Each respondent was interviewed according to a common schedule. First, he was asked to tell that fictional story, or stories, that in his opinion best characterized the Communist system, then he was questioned about his life and career under Communism, and, finally, his statements were checked against the "objective" information available on him. Every informant told several stories; altogether, they narrated one hundred fifty-six jokes, anecdotes, and short stories, a few examples of which will be presented in the following chapters. The second part of the interviews yielded many noteworthy comments, also quoted in the following chapters. The check on the informants seemed to be necessary and useful because people when interviewed are likely to put their best foot forward, even in an unrealistic way.

The respondents came from diverse backgrounds and had just as diverse personal characteristics. Some of them were former party members, others consistent opponents of the regime; some of them had suffered loss of freedom or other serious deprivations under Communism, others had managed to survive without calamities; some of them felt that religion was important to them, others were indifferent on this point. As a general rule, the informants did reveal one characteristic of their personality by telling stories in which a certain motif recurred more often than it would by pure chance.

The stories were all alike in rejecting Communism, but did so in different degrees and ways. If the reader compares the parable about the transformation of the nameless citizen (presented in Chapter II) with the anecdote about Károly, the student (to be found in Chapter X), he will immediately discern that the first one implies a severe, the second a relatively mild, rejection of Communism. The common rejection, then, is expressed in individual ways, and the stories can be easily classified by their motif or basic content into five categories.

First, there were some personal-background stories which presumably transferred a personal experience into fictional form; the story of the writer who could not write (Chapter XI) and "Forgive Me" (Chapter VIII) belong to this type.

Other stories, such as "Forgive Me" or the "Riot of the Clerks" told in Chapter IV, spoke of atrocities and emphasized the brutal character of Communism. A third group of stories were extrapunitive in their motif and contained the idea of aggression or threat of aggression against the Soviet regime or its representatives; the story of the party secretary and the flea (Chapter VII) and of the purged party member who hoped for the intercession of President Eisenhower (mentioned in Chapter X) are examples. Finally, some stories may be categorized as intropunitive because they contained the notion of self-abasement or abasement of other people who rejected Communism, such as the joke about the janitor (Chapter VI) and about the deaf lady who expected the American army (mentioned in Chapter X).

When the personal characteristics of the informants and the content of the stories were classified in this way, the resulting data were appropriate for statistical treatment.[4] The technical details and statistical results have been reported elsewhere.[5] In the present context it is sufficient to note some of the findings and interpret them according to their relevance for this study. Here are some findings:

The extent of personal suffering is not associated with the degree of the rejection of Communism. Thus, a person who suffered more is just as likely as one who suffered less to tell a story which rejects Communism mildly.

The former party member is somewhat more likely than the nonmember to tell atrocity stories and less likely to tell intropunitive stories. The former party member is as likely as the nonmember to reject Communism mildly or severely.

Informants who regard religion as important to them are more likely than other informants to tell stories of deprivation and frustration.

Informants whose personal motif is atrocity and extrapunition are more likely than other informants to tell stories severely rejecting Communism, while informants whose personal motif is deprivation-frustration are somewhat more likely than other informants to tell stories mildly rejecting Communism.

Informants whose personal motif is deprivation-frustration are more likely than the rest of the informants to tell personal-background stories.

If the results are examined in detail, it appears that certain characteristics are likely to occur together. Three such clusters of characteristics can be distinguished. In the first one are the relatively mild rejection of Communism, the special regard for the importance of religion, the motifs of deprivation and intropunition, and the personal-background stories. A second cluster is made up of the severe rejection of Communism and of the motifs of extrapunition and atrocity. And a third cluster is made up of membership in the party, the motif of atrocity, and the absence of the intropunitive motif. The extent of personal suffering does not appear in any of the clusters.

If we regard the stories as indicators of the attitude that the storyteller takes toward Communism, it is apparent that this attitude does not necessarily reflect his personal fortunes under the Soviet government. The personality rather than the experience itself is decisive in forming the attitude. One personality type which regards religion as important and shows a tendency for self-punishment is likely to see Communism as the source of deprivations and, yet, reject it mildly. Another personality type, which tends to see the Soviet world as the scene of atrocities and wishes to punish those perpetrating such brutal acts, is likely to reject Communism vehemently. There is, however, a third personality type rather similar to the second. This type, also, sees the Communist world as the scene of atrocities, but it is unwilling to punish itself or the party for the wrongs and perhaps feels a desire to participate in them. This personality type is likely to join the party.

It is possible to proceed with this interpretation by selecting the tendencies for self-punishment and punishment of others as the basic clues to the individual's attitude towards Communism. In this case one may argue that a person who reacts to the frustrations and vicissitudes of life with a tendency for self-punishment is likely to accept the deprivations of Communism and become an inconspicuous member of that gray mass which constitutes the majority of Soviet society. Another person who reacts to frustrations with a tendency for punishing others may become either an outspoken opponent of the Red system or a member of the party; and upon some further characteristics of his personality hinges the way he solves this dilemma and which of the two opposite poles he selects. But how free is he to choose one of the alternatives according to his own liking? What about the party, with its peremptory aim of changing the inner selves of the citizens? Does it not aim to multiply the personality that serves its purpose and suppress the other personalities?

The questions ask for the investigation of a complex social system. Having taken a small sample and a rather subjective method of interpretation, I have come a long way from my data; but the stories of the informants give certain suggestions which should be followed up. Now it is proper to have a look at the social system of Communism and at the reactions of the citizens to the system. This investigation may profit from my personal experiences and may fulfill the curiosity of my youth, but, I hope, it can be presented as the view of an unprejudiced observer.

II. THE MAKING OF THE SOVIET MAN

I

At the end of World War II, after bloody losses and fierce battles, the Soviet army stood far beyond the boundaries of the fatherland and held some seven European countries under its sway. It occupied an area stretching from the Baltic to the Black Sea and had extended its control, at least temporarily, out to the Mediterranean. The conquest of this territory—important to the domination of Europe—had been an ancient goal of Russian policy, pursued by the Czars with relentless determination through many wars of two centuries. Russian troops had repeatedly marched to these provinces, fought for them, and held them temporarily, without ever achieving a lasting rule over them.

This time, however, fate itself was favorable. The Nazi governments of the conquered countries vanished beyond recall, leaving behind them nothing but destruction, famine, and chaos. The Red Army arrived in a political vacuum, where nothing could challenge the conquerors in their efforts to shape and reshape the occupied territories. Indeed, the leaders of the Soviet Union had a clearly conceived plan—one might even call it a formula—about the future. They planned to keep the occupied provinces not simply by military force but by establishing Communism in them, by making them integral parts of the Communist empire. They set to work without delay and accomplished much within a few years. In each of those countries they installed the local Communist party as the sole wielder of power and leader of state and society; they reorganized the national economy according to the principles of the party and put ownership, production, and consumption under the tight control of the party state.

The political and economic changes, revolutionary as they were in the history of those seven peoples, amounted only to a partial fulfillment of the Communist formula. Something more had to be done, the accomplishment of which required many years of patient work but promised the farthest-reaching effects: the citizens of those countries had to be transformed into Soviet men.

These are vague words, but they express a fundamental tenet of Communism, which claims that its regime needs the support of a special kind of man who behaves according to Communist principles, conforms to the requirements of the party state, and is no more or less than a Soviet man. As soon as Bolshevism gained power in Russia, it began a grandiose educational experiment to produce Soviet men. It experimented in various ways at first, then worked out a general blueprint, and finally began production on a nation-wide basis. In the period from 1917 to 1945, the regime turned out its first generation of Soviet men. They grew up, were educated, worked, and lived under the omnipotent tutelage of the Communist system. By the end of that period the regime became convinced (if by no other proof than by its ultimate victory in the great war) that the blueprint was useful, effective, and correct.

Now the plan was to apply the same formula to the citizens of the freshly conquered countries, to form a second generation of Soviet man out of the Albanians, Bulgarians, Czechoslovaks, Germans, Hungarians, Poles and Rumanians. This was, in spite of the proved formula, a tremendous task, hedged about with many obstacles. The original Soviet man was created in the U.S.S.R., among Russians and other peoples who had lived under the influence of Russian culture and in an environment where the Communist idea had developed into a native phenomenon, devised by the native-born people and for the native-born. The second generation, however, had to be created out of seven non-Russian peoples, immensely nationalistic and proud of their national heritages, whose native cultures were different from, and even alien to, the Russian one. Up to this point, all but one of the seven peoples had had fiercely anti-Communistic, although dictatorial, governments; four of them spoke non-Slavic languages and could have no intercourse with the arriving Russian troops; and at least three of them had a long-standing hatred, and even contempt, for anything Russian.

Because of this diversity, many observers have been willing to label the Communist plan as chimerical. They have argued that language and national culture mark differences not only in politics but in human personality also; that a Hungarian, Romanian or Bulgarian, as long as he speaks his own language, will always differ from a Russian; that, consequently, the idea of the one and common Soviet mold is the unrealistic product of a doctrinaire mind. The Communist planners, however, were little concerned about academic arguments and just as little concerned about the significance of national diversity. They believed that the Hungarian or Bulgarian, as well as the Kazakh or Georgian, would with his peculiarities represent one variety of the same general species, the Soviet man.

The Communist plan, then, became a historical test. Success or failure in transforming seven individualistic peoples into the common mold of the Soviet man became the crucial test of the question whether or not Communism can be exported and established in non-Russian countries, whether it is for all peoples of the world, regardless of culture, creed, and fatherland, or whether it is strictly for those who happened to be born in Czarist Russia and the Soviet Union.

The leaders of Communism have never doubted that the first alternative is the correct one, but until the period after World War II they never had a chance to prove it. The Communist parties in Germany, France, and the U.S.A., militant and powerful as they were, had never gained power and never got in a position to make Soviet men out of the Germans, Frenchmen, and Americans. At that time, however, the chance came to prove before all observers, critics and sympathizers alike, that Communism has been right all the way and that human consistency can be effectively reshaped according to the doctrines of the party.

At this point, the plan became something like a psychological test, with implications even more formidable than the political implications. The making of the Soviet man (as it will be described in the following pages) is a kind of psychological manipulation, a high-grade, all-out human engineering that is directed towards changing people's "natural" psychological make-up according to a preconceived plan. This manipulation is not new in itself but has been used since time immemorial by many who possessed the power and opportunity to do so. Lately, however, it has become scientific, effective, and all-permeating as a result of the advances of technology in general and psychology in particular; and it has acquired even more these characteristics when it has been put to the service of the modern totalitarian state, this Leviathan of our century which can devote all the available means to that manipulation.

Present-day manipulation of human material has caused alarm even in democratic countries where the social forces of a free society check and balance the various manipulating powers. It has in totalitarian states evoked the opposition of almost everybody except the believers in that specific totalitarian creed. The particular Communist experiment, however, gave cause to much more alarm and fear than any other. If the second generation of Soviet man could successfully be produced according to a general formula, then here was the proof that the technique of psychological manipulation has become omnipotent and all-effective, that there remains no more room for the individual stand and personality, that mankind is ripe to fall into one common basket, like so many apples picked from the trees of an orchard.

These were the implications of the Communist experiment in seven countries, and this experiment will be the topic of the present book. I shall approach the topic with the method of social psychology and attempt to describe the general blueprint for producing Soviet men and its application to the masses of citizens. In this attempt I cannot avoid certain dangers and cannot, of course, claim infallibility. The Communist empire in its total extent is too big for one man's knowledge, and I claim to know only some parts and some aspects of it. Even so, official censorship and a lack of factual information pose many temptations to draw hasty conclusions and to color one's interpretations. My topic must be approached with a humility that recognizes the limitations of human knowledge. Yet I hope that the following study will contribute to a better understanding of the Communist system as well as of human manipulation in general.

II

One of those short stories which intellectuals behind the Iron Curtain pen in a solitary night hour and then hide in a locked drawer tells of a citizen who notices one morning that he has lost his head; the next morning he discovers the loss of his legs; the third morning, the disappearance of his arms; the fourth, of his heart. The fifth morning, when he is wondering how a man can live without head, legs, arms, and heart, he sees a sign reading "Marxism-Leninism" in the place of his head; another sign, "Agitation and Propaganda Department," instead of his legs; a third sign, "Soviet Work Competition," instead of his arms; a fourth one, "Party Discipline," instead of his heart. And on the seventh day, when he has to fill out one of those many forms which accompany life in a Communist state, he answers the question "Your Name" by putting down: "The Soviet Man."

Evidently, this bitter story is meant to express the political protest of a lonely intellectual. It speaks through rather crude symbolism and applies the metaphors of the folk tale to Communism, yet its meaning is clear and consistent. It describes how the citizen loses important parts of his self, and uses the popular words—head, legs, arms, and heart, to symbolize what the psychologist would call the superego. The story asserts that the citizen loses what is the central guidance in all his actions, the psychological source of his principles, norms, and goals. He loses that part of himself which stimulates him to realize ideals, which controls him, compares his actions to his cherished norms, fills him with satisfaction or dissatisfaction, and metes out inner rewards and punishments.

The artificial signs and fancy names that our citizen receives in exchange for the lost part of himself symbolize the total guidance of the party, the collective superego of Communism, that he accepts from necessity. This transformation makes him a Soviet man, one nameless element of the mass. At this point, the story becomes plausible, it can be explained in general psychological concepts.

Every man has to live with his individual superego. Were he alone in the world, doing so would not present any great problem. However, he depends for his life on others and has to live in groups. Each group has a collective superego, a system of goals, values, norms, and rules acknowledged by the membership. A country club has etiquette; a fishing party, an organized division of labor; a juvenile gang, rules of loyalty, binding upon all members. The large groups thoughtfully elaborate their norms and entrust them to writing; they have their ideology, philosophy, ethos or law.

In every group, man encounters norms which are not of his own making, yet he has to abide by them. The collective superego spells out duties and requires devotion. Man responds to it; he fulfills the duties through his work and shows devotion, for example, through his participation in rituals. Who fulfills the requirements, feels satisfied; who falls short of the measure, feels tension, anxiety, frustration. In this way the superego gives out its own rewards and punishments and sets human conscience into motion.

Through membership, a person accepts the norms of the group as a part of his individual superego; in other words, he "internalizes" them. By doing so, he identifies himself with the group, his goals and values with those of the group. He still remains an individual, but co-operates with other members in the common work and ritual. Some people co-operate sincerely and eagerly, others more or less reluctantly. Identification with a group occurs in many degrees, and while one person is very superficially identified with the common values, another one is willing to sacrifice his life for them. Those who seem to follow the superego most perfectly usually become the leaders of the group.

Man has to satisfy both the individual and the collective superego, and it is no small task to serve two masters. The collective superego may make a demand which is contrary to his individual norms, it may severely restrict his freedom to pursue his own goals, it may require much self-sacrifice and abnegation. Nevertheless, people readily identify themselves with a group and submit to the burdens of common norms. They do so because thereby they expect to gratify some of their basic needs. Man needs protection against enemies, needs prestige among his fellow beings, and these needs and many others can be satisfied in groups only. In order to achieve their gratification, people are willing to adhere to exacting norms. A greater need or more gratification leads to a closer identification, in some cases to a highly emotional involvement in the group.

The followers of a superego differ among themselves. Some of them are leaders, others are greatly involved, and still others poorly identified; however, the common work and ritual require their systematic co-operation. Hence, an organization grows up around the superego (such as the state and the church) and binds all members with strong ties to the common principles. It teaches and propagates the norms, it increases the general devotion to them. In particular, it tries to influence and supervise the members, persuade and command them to be faithful.

Within a large organization many groups and superegos exist side by side, and the individual may put himself into relation to any number of them. The national society of America contains many social classes and religious, ethnic, and occupational groups, and so many clubs and associations that their number is beyond count. The average American is often faced with the necessity of selecting some superegos and rejecting others. Seemingly, he lives in a maze of contradictory goals and values, and his plight is confusion and indecision. Still, a certain system exists for him. Some groups have a more powerful and more complete superego, others a weaker and more limited one. Using the distinction made by the sociologist C. H. Cooley, we may speak of primary and secondary groups. The first ones, represented by family, church, and nation, are established in the natural course of life, through informal, affective, stable ties. The secondary groups, represented by clubs, civic organizations, business firms, are formed voluntarily for the pursuit of a definite goal, and people join or leave them according as their own interest conforms to or varies from the common interest of the group.

The primary group develops a superego somewhat unintentionally during the natural group life. The members adopt it incidentally by being exposed to it from birth and learning it in the early years of life. Although its norms are often unwritten, they are well understood and have a lasting influence. The secondary group, on the other hand, forms its rules with conscious deliberation in order to further the common aim. Thus, it can set up norms only within the limited range of common interest. Although the rules are often formally announced in a charter or constitution, their function is subordinate to the function of the rules of the primary groups.

The case of political parties may serve as a good example to illustrate our somewhat abstract discussion. The basic principle of democracy regards man as an autonomous agent who is free to select his superego. It regards the political party as a secondary group that is subordinate to other, primary groups and that represents the *political* aspirations and opinions of its voters but no other. Hence, the political party cannot regulate the whole range of life but one segment only. It can have but a few compulsory norms and has to leave nonpolitical problems to other groups or to the voluntary decision of the individual. It asks for a limited identification and permits the citizen to change his political affiliation any time.

On the other hand, the totalitarian parties deny personal autonomy and try to impose a full-blown superego of their own creation upon all the citizens. Wherever they exist, they claim the rights of a primary group; as a matter of fact, they equate themselves with primary groups: the Nazi party with the mythical *Volkstum,* the Communist party with the equally mythical "proletarians of the world." There is always something faked and bogus about totalitarian parties —if nothing else, their exaggerated claims, promises, and programs that trespass on all fields of life. Such programs require severe sanctions. The totalitarian party commands its subjects to accept its norms, to identify intensely, and to renounce all other identifications. It wants to establish a monopoly in goals, values, and power.

At present, the totalitarian claim is conspicuously embodied in the Communist party. It claims to be more than it is; it claims to be the first and foremost primary group, the miraculous mixture of a super-nation, -religion, and -family. It prescribes a full set of norms and demands complete identification. It demands that everybody should be transformed by the party and fitted into the Communist mold. It demands that everybody should live by Communist rules and disown all other norms, that everybody should be nothing but a Soviet man and should totally identify himself with the political system. This demand is the essence of Communism, the strength and weakness of the party, the very feature that poses the gravest problems to all its subjects.

III. THE RED SUPEREGO

THE HISTORY OF Bolshevism began with a debate among a few *émigrés* on what seemed to be a petty issue: how to word the first paragraph of the statement of principles of the All-Russian Social Democratic Labor party. On this point Lenin split the party into two factions and, soon, into two parties; he put this point above unity, the cherished dream of illegal political movements. The main issue between Lenin and Martov was, indeed, more important than the phrasing of a paragraph defining party membership and more fundamental than the question of whether the aim should be a mass party or an élite party. A distant observer in the Caucasus comprehended the real nature of the issue, and young Stalin came out with a pamphlet in support of Lenin. "The party members," wrote Stalin, "will be able to carry on the struggle and apply the party's views only if they unite into a monolithic organization. . . . Only those can be regarded as members of this party who work in this organization, and who therefore consider it their duty to merge their wishes with those of the party and to act at one with the party. . . . Only by joining one of the party organizations and thus merging our personal interests with the interests of the party can we become members of the party."[1]

Lenin and Stalin broke away from the basically democratic principles of the Social Democratic Party. They planned a monolithic organization and demanded that every member should merge his wishes and interests with those of the party, should accept the norms and values of the party as his superego, and should realize them according to his abilities. When the revolution of 1917 put that monolithic organization into power, the basic requirement of complete identification was extended to all subjects who came to live under the domination of the party.

I

The demand originated with Lenin, the obstinate rebel. He announced it in one of his early writings: "We must train people who shall devote to the revolution not only their spare evenings, but the whole of their lives."[2] The revolutionist is, as a matter of fact, a common human type, one who repudiates the traditional superego of his milieu and tries to overthrow it. Young Lenin revolted, perhaps against the authority of his father to whose black chair in the library he had been relegated as the usual punishment of his childhood. He revolted against the milieu represented by his father, the devout, respectable, conservative school inspector enrolled in the ranks of minor nobility. At the age of sixteen, when "he perceived clearly that there was no God, he tore the cross violently from his neck, spat upon it contemptuously, and threw it away."[3] It is of no great import whether this episode is a fact or a fabrication of the official propaganda organs—it sums up a characteristic trait. Still an adolescent, Lenin theatrically denied the superego of the parental home. The significance of a theatrical gesture should not be overestimated. Adolescent revolts occur every day and are appeased just as often with the coming of age. Once adolescence has passed, most people revert to their inherited norms and values. He who keeps the adolescent denial in adult age is the revolutionary. Lenin had a forceful motive to do so—the execution of his older brother for a plot against the life of the Czar.

Young Lenin had hardly passed through the stormy age of denial when he found an object of identification that emotionally compensated him for the renounced family milieu

—the Russian Social Democratic movement. To that one group he dedicated himself totally, focusing upon it the energy that people usually parcel out among many groups, family, church, occupation, class, national society. For him the party performed the services of all other groups. He lived in the party and for the party. Instead of becoming a lawyer, he became a party man. Finally, having split the Social Democrats, he realized his desire: he and his party became one and the same thing.

His revolt was a unique, subjective, and somewhat mystical experience, but Lenin tried to repress its real origin. He set up his individual revolt as a general revolution of all peoples, one determined by historical necessity, and claimed that his own superego was in fact a collective superego that had to be accepted by everybody. He denied all the personal elements of his experience and posited it as an objective, "scientific" theory. As he began to organize the party, to recruit and initiate new members, the reasons to deny his personal involvement became even more compelling. He had to present himself not as a rebel against his environment looking for an ideology but as the fulfillment of the Marxist philosophy. Thus, he expressed his experience, to a great extent, in terms of the concepts of Marx and Engels, with whom he was willing to identify himself. The result came to be called the Communist philosophy.[4]

Identification with a person does not necessarily mean a sincere and consistent acceptance of all his ideas. The identification may be with an image, and it is the fate of many heroes that they are turned into images and worshiped in more or less idealized forms. The identification with Marx and Engels did not result in the correct incorporation of their teachings into Communist philosophy. As a matter of fact, their contribution was more important in some abstract tenets than in practical policy. The practical policy of Communism came from quite a different source: from those Russian traditions of autocratic power which through the Czars go back to the Byzantine Empire, from there to Diocletian and, in the final analysis, to Oriental despotism. The Byzantine historian Procopius, who wrote his *Secret History* of Emperor Justinian in the sixth century, gives a better insight into actual life under Communism than Marx's *Capital* or Engels' *Family, Private Property, and the State*.

Few humans are able to tear themselves out of their native surroundings. Even revolutionaries accept some parts of the collective superego of their environment. Lenin was no exception. He did not reject all the norms and values of native Russia; the country was much bigger than the parental milieu. He denied what his father stood for but sincerely accepted many native Russian ideas. He made them a relevant part of Communism and created, thus, a creed of basically Oriental origin.

II

Any collective superego that wants to perpetuate itself has to face a fundamental problem. It must decide who has the right to formulate the official tenets, who has the right to teach. If the office of teaching is not regulated, if anybody is permitted to discuss and resolve the cardinal problems, diverse and contradictory tenets may be espoused and the whole superego may crumble. The issue was clearly settled in the early years of the Bolshevik party. The Communist philosophy represented Lenin's personal needs and desires, norms and goals; therefore, Lenin had the sole right of expounding it in the orthodox way. Lenin, however, repressed his personal involvement and established a strong organization, the party, around his superego. He entrusted the party with the task of announcing and guarding the superego, of persuading and commanding all people to be faithful. In order to carry out this task, the party had to exercise a total power over all members and all subjects.

In the name of the party, Lenin, of course, was himself the teacher and interpreted the norms in terms of his personal experience. In this way the apocalyptic character of the Communist philosophy was established. Lenin, and later his successors, revealed as much of the Communist lore as it appeared practical to divulge under the given circumstances. They did not reveal more than this, and never revealed the entire lore. The content of the whole superego has never been collected in a systematic way and put into the hands of the subjects. The tenets have never been expounded in a *System,* but only in pamphlets, speeches, and editorials. Such short pieces, written in a semi-popular style, have explained what the public should know—certain selected chapters of official teachings.

After Lenin, Stalin achieved the supreme office of power and teaching. As a theoretician, Stalin does not fare badly when compared to some of his contemporaries, to Hitler, Mussolini, and a score of minor dictators who have now passed into oblivion; nevertheless, he was inexperienced in the teachings of the classical authors of socialism. Under his tenure as chief teacher, the Marxist elements of Communist philosophy were further thinned out, to be replaced by Russian ideas. Under Stalin Communism was pushed further away from its Western forefathers. One may believe Trotsky's judgment that Stalin was never interested in theoretical problems beyond their immediate practical use. Stalin, busy with the daily tasks of administration, restricted himself to occasional explanations of current policy problems, given mainly in his reports to the party congresses. He delegated his authority in teaching to the ranking members of the party bureaucracy.

Kaganovich, Vyshinsky, Zhdanov, and the other bureaucrats who were entrusted with this authority did not comprehend the revolutionary experience of Lenin; they made an impersonal ideology out of what originally had been the personal creation of Lenin. They restricted themselves to the current questions of daily importance, which were treated in a matter-of-fact way but always with a seasoning of vague, ritualistic references to the Marx-Engels philosophy as the alleged basis of the announcements. These ideological bureaucrats spoke with the voice of those who possess the power and are addressing those who are their subjects. The acceptance of their propositions was enforced not by reasoning but by the power of the party state. The propositions were, for all practical purposes, administrative orders of the state, executed like laws and *ukazes*.

The speeches and writings of Lenin were intended to conquer and enrapture the masses. Bureaucratic announcements do not have such a far-reaching aim. They are presented everywhere in the special stylistic garb of officialese. In the hands of the bureaucrats, Communist philosophy assumed that official style, devoid of individualism and similar to the style of state laws. The theoretical manifestos are unreadable; they are dull, dry, lifeless, and as ritualistic as the mosaic of Byzantine art. Their masses of platitudes can be judged by the titles of some rather important items: "The Russian People—Leading Force among the Peoples of Our Country," "The Education of the Young Communists—One of the Fundamental Tasks of the Party Organizations," "Intensify the Ideological-Political Work of the Party Organizations," "Tirelessly Raise the Ideological-Theoretical Level of the Party-Soviet Cadres," "Leninism—The Most Advanced World View," "Indestructible Is the Might of the Stalinist Bloc of Communists and Non-Party Men."[5]

Communist philosophy is elaborated not by philosophers but by political practitioners. The authority of teaching is intertwined with the authority of running the political machine. The Soviet leaders have one qualification for teaching: their possession of power. As one would expect, they announce a philosophy that serves their momentary political interest. Their statements, as critics have often pointed out, show logical shortcomings and contradictions, but internal consistency or flawless reasoning are really irrelevant to them. Perhaps no superego has ever been entirely logical in its structure and flawless in its presentation.

The leaders produce the Communist philosophy during their hectic struggles for power. When making a pronouncement, they have the obligation to identify themselves with the party, and they have their own political aims as well—to preserve and enhance, within the party, their own power. They make the announcement that is most appropriate in a given situation. As the process is officially described, "The propaganda of Marxist-Leninist theory which our party tirelessly carries on . . . is always subordinated to the basic tasks confronting the party at this or that historical stage."[6] These occasional propagandistic proclamations, put forward in a loose and haphazard way, make up the philosophy. Every practical instruction given by the party becomes a part of the philosophy and carries the same weight as any of the abstract doctrines; as a matter of fact, the practical instructions crowd out the philosophical tenets. The resulting body of teachings, a mass of superficial, watered-down, and ambiguous platitudes, does not make a philosophical system in the academic sense of the word. It is an ideology manufactured for the purpose of serving the power system; it is a body of vague principles by which the leaders justify whatever actions they take; it is, therefore, imposed from above, established, ordered, and directed by the state and party.

Small wonder that Communist philosophy is forever changing. It is the rationalization of the party's policy and must regularly be adjusted to the momentary requirements of power politics. A democratic party can easily redefine its aims and means when the actual situation changes; it can alter its policy without loss of prestige. The totalitarian philosophy of Communism cannot admit changes but has to proclaim that both the old and new policy are integral parts of the original philosophy, that the change is inherent in the philosophy. This tour de force can be accomplished with the aid of the dialectical method.

In Hegel's and Marx's hands, dialectic was used within the perspective of the philosophy of history, and though it was perhaps not a very useful tool in explaining history, it was still a manageable abstract concept. The Communist theoreticians gave a practical twist to it and pulled it down to the level of pettifoggery. Bukharin still kept dialectic on a philosophical plane when he declared, "The dialectic method of interpretation demands that all phenomena be considered in their indissoluble relations."[7] But its current use in the personal struggle of the party is more sophisticated. "For the Marxists," wrote *Pravda,* "theory has never been a goal in itself, but a means, the most important form of the great struggle of the working class. Marxism, as Lenin teaches, enables us to determine what policy we should follow under the given circumstances."[8]

The relationship in which the phenomena are considered is their bearing upon the interest of the party, and dialectic serves to rationalize the tactical changes of daily politics. At this point it loses any philosophical relation and turns into political sophistry. Bertolt Brecht, describing with rare frankness the petty dialectic, mixes the tone of loyalty with parody :

> Who fights for Communism, should be able to
> fight and not to fight,
> he should say the truth and yet not the
> truth,
> serve and deny service,
> keep a promise and break it,

take any danger and avoid it,
be known and be unknown.[9]

Dialectical or not, the inconsistent changes in the teaching cannot escape the attention of the subjects. As one of my informants put it: "Every morning one has to read the newspaper to learn what the party teaches today." The official philosophy changes, sometimes suddenly, and the party demands the immediate acceptance of the new tenet. No delay is permitted. Those who are late in their acceptance are severely criticized, for example, in the following terms: "There are comrades who have come to a sudden stop now, when, as a result of the new regrouping, they are faced with new tasks. Often they rigidly cling to their old conceptions. . . . We must take severe measures against them. . . . They must overcome that resistance which hinders the realization of the resolutions of the Central Committee and the program of the government."[10]

A person seldom identifies himself with a new proposition at a moment's notice. It takes time to incorporate a new idea into the individual superego, and a sudden change in the teachings evokes resistance or skepticism among the subjects. Neither response is compatible with the demands of the party, and both must be suppressed. Instead, the subject must feel that the party is always right but that he himself is ignorant, laggard, recalcitrant; he is an obstinate procrastinator who resists the truth. Thus, any tour de force of dialectic, any change in the teaching, fills the subjects with the feeling of uneasiness, unworthiness, inferiority; and those feelings in the masses are obviously not disapproved of by the leaders. They are, indeed, systematically instilled into the people.

III

It is the duty of the leaders to announce the superego, and the duty of the Soviet men to accept it. One leader, addressing the new members of the party, reiterated the old commonplace once more: "It is our task of vital importance to turn the party into a truly monolithic organization in which every single member is imbued with the same spirit, led by the same desire and the same will. It is imperative that the comrades . . . quickly master the theory of Marxism-Leninism and accept the iron discipline of the party."[11] How many politicians and civic leaders have harangued about the sameness of desires and will. In the mouth of Communist teachers, however, this is not a cheap cliché but a rigorous belief, a realistic program. They claim that the Communist philosophy is all-embracing and contains the answers to all possible questions; that it is right and gives the only correct answer in every case; that since it is complete and valid, it must be accepted by all subjects; and that it must be accepted fully as it is announced.

"Guided by the mighty Marxist method," expounded Mikoyan at the Twentieth Congress of the party, "the Central Committee clarifies the contemporary events of social development, explains them in a Marxist way, and arms the working man with conclusions which generalize and explain . . . events both in capitalist and socialist countries."[12] The Communist philosophy claims somewhat more—to offer all the norms and values that should regulate life. Nothing is excluded from its range. It rules over power politics, economics, and intellectual pursuits; it directs literature, architecture, music, and dance. It bids for the faithful services of science and scholarship, of history (the usual meretrix of political regimes), of biology, and of folklore. A Communist linguistics as well as statistics must exist in sharp contrast to bourgeois pseudo-science.[13] The Red philosophy must regulate the private lives of individuals, their love and marriage, their etiquette, their work and recreation. Once, the traditions of the Graeco-Roman world sharply separated the public and private spheres of life, and the old Roman did not permit the *res publica* to interfere with the private life of his windowless home. Oriental despotism was never fastidious on this point, and Communism has wiped out any dividing line between public and private. Its ideal family is but an extended cell of the party.

Every problem, every action, every detail of private or communal life must be referred to the party and decided accordingly. Each is a "political" question, and politics must penetrate everything. One theoretician declared: "We must develop a socialist architectural style." A party functionary lectured to a group of musicians: "Even a viola gamba solo can be played in the Soviet way." The director of an opera house declared: "We shall not tolerate the falsification of Beethoven by reactionary groups." The manager of a state enterprise addressed the recently hired draftsmen: "The line you draw makes politics."[14]

The human mind is imperfect, and its knowledge is limited. The theses actually promulgated by Communist philosophy fall short of omniscience. Those questions that the official philosophy is unable to answer must be ignored or repressed, their existence denied, and their names removed from the dictionary. A totalitarian philosophy gives a one-sided picture of the world. It represses many ideas and experiences; it never makes a straightforward statement; it can never cope with logical arguments. It cannot tolerate spontaneity; it is full of inhibitions. With its half-statements and broken ideas, it is redolent of the speech of pathologically inhibited people who never finish their sentences.

Communist philosophy, nevertheless, claims to be able to decide all questions beyond doubt, in a simple yes-or-no way; to contain all the "right" answers, valid for any person, at any time and in any place; to be the only correct philosophy, perfect and infallible. These totalitarian claims have two enemies—the facts and the other theories.

Communist theory is stronger than the facts, and facts cannot refute it. If any contradictory facts are found, they must be erroneous, must be ignored or adjusted to the theory. This contempt for facts is responsible for many failures of Soviet economy and foreign policy. On the other hand, any demand of the superego must be regarded as a fact, and this reification of the demand accounts for a strange ideality about Communist announcements that is frequently regarded by Western observers as "lying." Since the demand is that every subject must identify himself with the party, his identification is a fact beyond doubt. Indeed, political elections in the Soviet countries have no other purpose than to demonstrate the repeated satisfaction of the demand by invariably yielding almost 100 per cent of the votes to the regime.

If facts can be defeated so easily, the fight against the competing theories must require even simpler administrative measures. No other superego can be legitimate, and every person or organization must agree with the party. The non-Communist philosophies must be discarded and individual deviations eradicated. Any contradictory or critical statement must be wrong, superfluous, and harmful, and must be prohibited. No criticism of the Red superego is permitted. The party can, and does, criticize everybody, but nobody should criticize the party.

Any organization that professes another superego must be suppressed, because "water and fire do not mix."[15] In order to preserve its unmixed purity, Bolshevism makes a total war against the competing superegos. Religion and nationalism are the two main targets, and the authority of the church to set up norms and values must be fought in the same way as the effects of patriotism, which makes man identify himself with his native country rather than with the party. Communism does not overlook the lesser foes either, and all organizations representing democratic ideas have been suppressed, as well as the Boy Scout movement and the Rotary Club of the satellite countries.

Not even love, the most venerable form of identification, is permitted to compete with the monopoly of Communism. The dangers of love are evident: lovers are identified with each other, not with a political movement, and the family is more concerned with its own values and goals than with those of the collective superego. Communism fights love not in its erotic but in its spiritual form and applies the tactics of the party to the most intimate of human relationships. The party has no objection to sexual satisfaction, if it is obtained within the limits set up by the Red morality, although the French Communist Party warned members against pretty women who might interfere with their work.[16] However, the party frowns upon emotional involvement in love, because emotions unite the lovers and drive them away from the political movement. The party, by no means incidentally, disrupts family life all too often. Members are, under certain circumstances, advised or ordered to leave their families and, should duty call, may not even be permitted to go to the deathbed of their nearest kin.[17]

Since one constantly has to be at the disposal of the party, one should not be too much in love, should never be involved above the matter-of-fact level. One informant told me the story of a young party secretary who was transferred to another city. He had just retired to his room after the first day's hard work when the door opened and an attractive girl entered. "Comrade," she said, "I have come to fulfill my duties." The heroes of the Communist screen, stage, and press sacrifice their love to the party without hesitation. The ideal Communist may have love affairs and may enter a conventional marriage, but the party must come first and loved ones after it.[18]

The party ruthlessly eradicates all organizations with

competitive superegos, but the control of conscience requires more than that. A church, a party, a club may be crushed, but people's loyalty may survive. Communism, accordingly, has developed a special technique to deal with divided loyalties. It claims that everybody must open his mind to receive the truth of the Red philosophy. Any person who shuts his mind to the Communist truth must be animated by evil intentions. He is branded an "enemy of the people," an expression that was coined during the Russian civil war and has become one of the most frequently used words of the Communist vocabulary. There is not much logic in the definition of "enemy." Every critic and dissenter is an enemy. Humanity is divided into two opposing camps—the faithful and the enemy.

According to the Communist view, the world is populated with an incredibly great number of enemies, endowed with the malevolence and power of demons and bent on the destruction of the Red system. More numerous and more ferocious than King James's famous crew, they assail the party unremittingly, and against them "we cannot insure ourselves through locks."[19] One official manifesto enumerates the following kinds of Communist demons: the Western imperialistic circles, the *ancien régime,* aristocracy, clerical reaction, right-wing Social Democrats and other democratic parties, the revisionist faction of the Communist party, capitalists, fascists, gendarmes, anarchists of *petit bourgeois* leanings, and kulaks and other reactionary elements of the countryside.[20] This motley of evil spirits gathers in Walpurgis Nights to concoct plots against Communism.

The fury of these faceless demons must be met with an equal fury from the party. They must be exorcised not with spiritual but with physical weapons. Totalitarian parties cannot fight competition with the spiritual weapons of peaceful discussion, persuasion, and compromise. Their fight takes place not on the platform but in Mauthausen and Vorkuta. Communism calls upon the muscular strength of party members to ferret the enemies out of their hiding places and annihilate them mercilessly. Only "the utter defeat of the political and ideological positions of these enemies" will strengthen Communism.[21]

The physical annihilation of the demons is not enough. Their harmful spirit and ideas also have to be extirpated. Censorship is necessary in every totalitarian system, as a part of the general war against the competing superegos. Ideas contrary to the teachings of the party must not be tolerated. "The revolutionary worker-peasant government," declares one official paper, "must not tolerate the poisoning of souls. It has not, and will not in the future either, permit our press to be used against the real interest of the people."[22]

In a free society the individual may select from among the many collective superegos. A democratic party never expects that everybody will adopt its program; it is content if the majority of the voters give their approval. The Soviet system, however, claims that "the masses of people wish to follow the directives of the party."[23] In fact, this is not a matter of wishing but of obeying. Communist philosophy must be accepted by all subjects, everybody must open his heart before its teachings. We may believe the reports coming from Soviet sources that kolkhoz workers read Marx and Lenin, that sales girls discuss Makarenko and Lysenko; they do so under orders.

Every collective superego tends to propagate itself and transmit its teachings to new disciples and future generations. It makes itself fully available to the attentive students and instructs all those who are interested in learning. The Communist party copiously expounds the teachings but subordinates this communication to its political interest. Communist philosophy is manipulated by the leaders; it is, in turn, announced or revised, apportioned or withheld, as the need may arise. The interest of political power is not furthered by complete and equal knowledge on the part of all of the subjects. The masses are supposed to know not the whole system but only those tenets that are tactically useful; and only a handful who are nearest the highest echelons are permitted to gain a full knowledge. "The voluntary nature of party education," explains one source, "does not imply that the party organizations can leave it to the decision of incidental circumstances who should and who should not study." No, knowledge must be distributed in a hierarchical order. Those in the higher ranks should know more, the masses only the necessary minimum. The Central Committee of the Hungarian party ruled that "irresponsible nominations to party schools must cease."[24]

The party teaches only a selected group and only to the extent suggested by political expediency. Every young man who is thirsty for knowledge and eager to study for study's sake encounters these restrictions on teaching and is barred from the full body of knowledge. One young intellectual who attended, successively, an introductory party seminar of six lectures, then a full-time six-week course, followed by a four-month session at a party academy, topped by two years at the Marx-Lenin Institute, worded his disillusionment in this way: "At each stage the teacher told us somewhat apologetically that more of the subject would be taught at the next stage. There we got more words but not more ideas. At the end of it, my thirst was as unquenched as at the beginning. Either I had to shut my mind and believe that there was a Communist philosophy somewhere beyond our intellectual reach, or I had to let my mind work and conclude that there was no such animal as a Communist philosophy." Inquisitiveness does not help either, since it meets only icy silence. "I asked many questions," complained Howard Fast, "not one of which was answered."[25]

The haphazard haziness of the official announcements,

the degrees of secrecy of the study, are not incidental shortcomings. Except for a few leaders, nobody knows exactly what the correct answers should be. The student is deprived of the freedom to do his own research, to clear up the doubtful points, to compare the contradictory passages, to fill out the lacunae. He gropes around insecurely in the darkness of ignorance, expecting directives from the party leaders. He becomes dependent upon the leaders, as if tied through his whole life by an umbilical cord. Dimly he feels that the leader must know and will surely announce the answer in due time, that he himself is supposed to accept it when it comes and be a member of the obedient mass of eternal disciples.

On Easter Sunday, when American newspapers were editorializing on life triumphing over death, a Communist paper entitled its editorial, "Fidelity to Leninism Is the Foundation of Every Victory of the Communist Party."[26] The topic was not picked by caprice. "Fidelity" is a cardinal virtue of Red morality, demanding unbroken adherence to the superego. Every instruction of the party, however trivial it is, must be received with full loyalty. Production norms, speeches at the weekly meetings, and rearrangements of office hours must command the same enthusiasm. Life is full of "musts." The Red superego so vastly expands the realm of the compulsory that many voluntary actions may easily amount to faithlessness.

One must not make a selection among the tenets, one must not reject some of them. The partial acceptance of the superego is labeled deviation and sectarianism, which are punishable sins. The average subject wishes to avoid these errors, but he is hardly able to do so. The hazy structure of the Red philosophy gives rise to inadvertent sectarianism. People may fall into errors much against their will, just incidentally. The Soviet man, therefore, is eager to listen to his leader and to say neither more nor less than the leader. He echoes the leader word by word, quotes him as often as possible. It is most useful to know, by heart and ready for quotation, the appropriate passages of the official announcements—"citatology" is the word the Soviet countries use to describe this automatic reference to the dogma.

Fidelity and mimesis ensure adherence to the Communist philosophy. But how is it possible to accept the nonconscious part of the superego, which is never put into lucid concepts? Communism does not allow any concessions in this respect, but assigns the burden of the duty to the subject. The citizen must be constantly alert to find out the unspoken ideas of the leaders. He must perceive the nonconscious elements of the superego in the instructions given by the party; he must fulfill the instructions conscientiously and do as ordered. He must rigidly adhere to the discipline of the party, of the state, and of the police. Complete identification with the party is both cause and result of strict discipline. The masses must prove their loyalty by an obedient life that in its collectivistic aspects reminds one very much of the life of ants.

IV

The duty of the Soviet man is to accept the Red philosophy and identify himself with the party; as a matter of fact, he is not supposed to appear as an individual but as a representative of the party. In formal statements he is supposed to avoid the pronoun "I" and speak of "we Communists." But words are not enough; identification must be demonstrated in deeds. It must be manifested in that collective behavior in which the personality disappears in the "communism" of the ant-like crowd.

A general approval of the superego represents but the lowest degree of identification. The woman Klimenko (the first person the reader meets in Konstantine Simonov's novel *Days and Nights*) can talk of nothing but her fixed idea—the rebuilding of Stalingrad after the war. This simple and somewhat factual identification is becoming to plain people who cannot do any better. For them, it is enough to approve enthusiastically the resolutions of the party as if they represented the universal consensus of all citizens.

A somewhat higher degree of identification establishes an identity of feelings. The party's joys and sorrows are the subject's joys and sorrows; the party's triumphs are his triumphs; and the party alone commands his attention and solicitude. As one example of the proper behavior, the kolkhoz worker, a widow in charge of six cows, is described as being happy because her cows thrive and the kolkhoz progresses; no reasons for unhappiness exist.[27] The identity of feelings must be supplemented by an identity of interests. The citizen is supposed to be a Jacques Bonhomme of Bolshevism who has no other thoughts and worries than the welfare of the party. The aftermath of one important political event in the Communist world was reported by the official press thus: "Many citizens of Moscow received with a shock the news about the anti-party plotting of Malenkov, Molotov, and Kaganovich. The shock turned into a powerful indignation. . . . A perfect unity of opinions exists. Whomever I address, everybody approves the decision of the Central Committee."[28] The party demands that the private interest be equated with the party's interest. What is good for the party should be good for the citizen, and we shall observe the application of this principle in the Communist ethic governing work.

These lower forms of identification, imperfect as they are, nevertheless require a certain self-sacrifice, and the idea of self-sacrifice has a central part in the Communist doctrines. Khrushchev described the people of the U.S.S.R. as "unafraid of difficulties and privations."[29] The statement, of course, refers to the party's demand and not to a voluntary decision of the subjects. The ethic of Western civilization leaves a great freedom to the individual in selecting the forms and fields of his self-sacrifice, but the Red superego commands an absolute self-sacrifice in the way that and at the time that the party requires it.

The perfect identification requires that the party should be more than one's life, that life should be sacrificed for the party. In Mother Bloor's words, "I should rather die than give up my active work with the party—to give it up would be death. I have been so much a part of the party that I cannot conceive of living in any sense without it."[30] The party strictly enforces this demand and sends many good Communists to certain death. One of them, sent to organize the party in a country where such organizational work was punishable by death, wrote after his capture, "I am a prisoner and I shall be executed in three days. My heart aches. My life will come to an end together with my illegal work for the party. I am equally sorry for my life and work since my life was filled with party work."[31] Comrade Rubashov, the best-known Communist of fiction, is described as one whose past, present, and future belong to the party.[32] One disillusioned Communist, looking back upon his wasted years, felt that the party demanded everything, "courage, poverty, self-sacrifice, discipline, intelligence, my life, and, at need, my death."[33]

The most perfect identification was tersely expressed by Kamenev when, at the point of his final defeat by Stalin, he declared, "We submit entirely and completely to the party."[34] What he says comes strikingly close to the complete submission demanded by fatalistic Mohammedanism, and the close meeting of two Oriental religions is perhaps not quite accidental. Whoever surrenders his own will to the party acknowledges that the party owns, and can dispose of, him in the same way as any person can own, and dispose of, an inanimate object. Indeed, the Communist system announces a totalitarian claim upon the individual, upon all individuals that the system can bring under its control. It claims and exercises an unrestricted authority over the entire physical and psychological make-up of its subjects and disregards any individual will. It acknowledges no other attitude than complete submission.

Communism is the dictatorship of a superego, persistent and ruthless in its claims. It does not care whether people like it or not; it poses demands with an utter disregard for the psychological reactions of the subjects. Is it, then, natural for the subjects to accept the demand for complete identification? Normally, I believe, the human being, following his nature, identifies himself with many groups and persons, distributes his identification among many claimants, and gains much satisfaction out of this diversity. He is happy when he can join a new group, but the Communist system deprives him of the freedom of multiple identification. His natural striving is frustrated, and the demand of undivided identification becomes a source of constant strain and tension.

The rigorous principles and harsh demands I have described so far are obviously deterrent rather than inducive; by themselves, they would produce few Soviet men indeed. A collective superego, however, consists not only of demands and principles but also of a technique of manipulating people and making them accept the demands—truly, faithfully, and without excessive psychological strains. The Communist system, in particular, has developed a manipulative technique that uses perhaps all the means that are available to change human beings according to a central plan. It offers generous rewards to those who sincerely conform. This central plan will be better understood if we investigate how the party state distributes its rewards through the commonest activities of daily life, through work and ritual.

IV. WORK AND RITUAL

THE RIOT OF THE CLERKS is the title one respondent gave to a story narrated to me. It tells of the sedulous clerks who work in an imaginary office and produce thick files from morning to night, without once lifting their heads from their papers. In time they prepare so many new files that the office gets cluttered and no room is left in which to store them. So one day the authorities decide to close down the useless office. They issue orders to this effect, but forget to assign new jobs to the old clerks. The scribes accept the order without a murmur, but, not knowing where to go, keep up their regular work. Every morning, sharply on time, they arrive in the office and produce new, useless files. Their activity becomes a public nuisance, a waste of work and paper, an open defiance of public order. The authorities feel compelled to take stern measures and despatch a regiment of soldiers to the scene. The clerks face the arms without flinching. They keep on working. Nothing but violence can quell them, and the soldiers have to do as commanded. The clerks are liquidated in their beloved office, receiving the deadly bullet in their chairs and with the final agonizing cramp of their hands still trying to finish the last useless file.

The weird, Kafkaesque tale is obviously concerned with duty. Duties, to be sure, are prescribed by every superego, and every superego requires that people should exert efforts, reach certain goals, and perform certain acts. "Our doctrine is not a dogma, but a guide to action," declared Lenin when he arrived in Russia to prepare the revolution.[1] This demand, like many other ones, must be interpreted in terms of totalitarian linguistics. It means that every subject must at all times exert his best efforts in order to realize the collective superego. In other words, the party describes all the duties, and the subjects have to obey. The duties are announced in the constitution, proclaimed in propaganda, and specified in those many instructions which are issued daily on almost every problem. They must be carried out meticulously, and any neglect calls for punishment. The ideal subject concentrates all his efforts upon the goals of the superego and does not squander energy on other aims. He is a monomaniac of duty, well symbolized in the scribes of our tale.

I

On February 24, 1917, an unknown tramcar conductor in St. Petersburg unexpectedly turned off his route, stopped the car, and told everybody to get off: "The car isn't going any farther." The passengers objected, scolded, but finally got off, and with this strike of the tramcar operators the Russian revolution started.[2] The action required courage, for the lonely conductor had to face the hostile passengers; it required timing and calculation of the risks involved. The strike succeeded because the unknown conductor was firmly determined to satisfy the requirements of his superego. His act was a demonstration, intended to call the attention of the public to his ideas. Such demonstrative action is always impressive, because it mobilizes the best abilities and utmost energies of the individual; it represents a momentous experience in life.

Single actions of this kind may be exciting and with their demonstrative aims may even achieve historical importance. But in ordinary life a superego is realized through less impressive activity, through systematic, routine work. The different superegos take their own attitudes towards work and evaluate it in their own terms. An "easy-going" superego may be unworried about the significance of work; a "rigorous" one may give it a place of central importance. The Red superego, being of the rigorous kind, is greatly preoccupied with the work of the subjects.

Communist morality demands that every able-bodied person should work, and the same demand is made by the "Protestant ethic" of America. But at this point the two ethics part and interpret the basic principle in quite different terms. Communist morality does not permit much freedom to the individual in selecting his work and haggling with an employer about wages and hours, it does not tolerate a leisure class, and it takes the lion's share of the fruits of work. It equates the individual's interest with the party's interest, but, after a strange arithmetical operation, the party's interest comes out with a higher value. The individual interest must always be subordinated to the "social" interest as embodied in the will of the party state. Since the state is the sole employer and high productivity at low cost is its best interest, every worker must contribute according to his abilities to this end.

"The workers shall contribute," the constitution of the Hungarian People's Republic declares, "to the establishment of socialism by their labor, by their participation in socialistic work competition, by raising discipline and perfecting work methods."[3] The citizen has to labor self-sacrificingly; he cannot have the right to select his work, but gets his occupation, place, and conditions of work assigned by the authorities. Wherever he is put, he must be satisfied and work assiduously. Armies of workers have been sent into Arctic regions, into the Siberian wilderness, into dangerously primitive mines and forced labor camps to haul timber, extract ore, build new plants, and increase the productive capacity of the country. Those armies, through their life, work and death, fulfilled their duty as it was defined for them by the party.

The work of the citizens is co-ordinated and applied for the benefit of the political regime through state planning, a conspicuous feature of the Soviet economy. The planning of private enterprises in America serves the final aim of a capitalistic economy, the maximization of profits. Planning is done by the management of each enterprise in order to prepare the future conditions that will yield higher profit: increased production, more efficient sales promotion, and greater customer satisfaction.

In Communism the leadership of the party state manages all enterprises, and state planning originates with the highest leadership of the regime, with those people who have the authority to teach. The planners often ignore efficiency and satisfaction, but pursue quite a different aim: the realization of the Red superego. Planning goes far beyond economic life and covers not only production, consumption, and investment but also education, sports, arts, recreation, and many other fields. It includes slum clearance in a city, road building in a county, the annual program of a sport club and theater, and the activities of the Academy of Sciences.

The master plan outlined by the leaders sets certain general targets for the total production of the country. Then the plan is broken down by the branches of economy, within the branches by production units, within the plants by departments, and within the departments by workers. Every worker has his own plan, centrally assigned; the authorities prescribe a certain work norm that he has to fulfill. The duties assigned by state planning, like moral duties in general, cannot ever be finally discharged. If a goal is reached, a new one must be set. "For us Bolsheviks," Stalin declared, "the five-year plan is not something finished and given once and for all. . . . [It is] a first approximation, which must be made more exact, changed, and completed on the basis of experience."[4] While engaged in fulfilling the norms of the state, the Soviet man cannot develop a personal plan of his own. He cannot plan for himself in matters of work, income, and saving because the state may tear down all private plans with one stroke. The citizen has but a passive role in state planning: to respond to the central hand as it pushes the button.

Work is an inexhaustible source of satisfaction, provided it is approved by the individual superego. It may give direct satisfaction arising from the fulfillment of duty, from a sense of the value of labor itself, or from the qualities of the product fabricated through work. Again, it may give indirect satisfaction through the money earned and through the many things that money can buy. In a way which is by no means incidental, capitalism tends to over-emphasize the monetary rewards, while Communism, the direct satisfaction.

The Soviet system holds out a great many non-monetary rewards and uses them to fill the workers with as much direct satisfaction as possible. It claims that the Soviet worker, being free from the exploitation of capitalists, works for himself and his comrades, works for a brighter future and a better world. In addition, the Soviet system attempts to combine the offices, shops, and plants with welfare institutions, with cafeterias, recreational centers, nurseries, and schools, some of which measure up to high standards indeed and appeal greatly to the workers. Its policy is that the workers should regard the office or shop as a sort of second home, as something that is approached with loving sentiments. The effects of this policy must not be underestimated. After all, words and sentiments are essential parts of man's work, and through such means the party state consistently endeavors to give a real meaning to the work of the citizens.

At the same time, however, the centralized planning of individual duties disregards the indirect satisfactions and makes some precarious assumptions. It assumes that all citizens define duty in the same way as the party defines it for them. It denies the legitimacy of individual plans. The gigantic targets of state planning do not leave room for the small goals of an individual, and the desire for a home, a car, or an appliance must be sacrificed to build the Magnitogorsk combine and the Turkmenian Canal. Although the situation has been greatly improved under the Khrushchev regime, the citizen is still supposed to renounce the daily comfort given by the various consumer goods in order to build up heavy, and particularly military, industry.

The renunciation of monetary satisfaction, as demanded by Communism, represents a grave problem in the seven satellite countries. The first generation of Soviet man was produced among the peoples of Russia who lived in a backward economy, had few pretensions, and did not know of those many goods that were available to the masses in the capitalistic countries of the West. The second generation, however, had to be created among peoples who were more or less affected by the spirit of capitalism and were well aware of all those things that money can buy. As one informant put it, the *muzhik* of the Czar worked out of tradition, but the peasant in Hungary and Germany worked to get ahead.

Hence, the workers in the satellite countries are more likely than the workers in the U.S.S.R. to resent the assignment of duties and the scarcity of consumer goods. The former are likely to feel that the goals of the state plan are not their own and that the production norms are not commensurate to wages. Small wonder that the norm system, that logical corollary of state-assigned duties, is the center of stormy protests coming from two sides. The authorities complain of the laxity of the workers. The workers grumble just as often that the norms are too high and the pay too low; that they do not get more money for more production; that it is not worthwhile to produce more. One informant, elaborating on this problem, pointed to the psychology of the workers: "Take our factory. The fellows there work to fulfill the plan. Then comes a party secretary with sweet talk, and the fellows work more. Another secretary comes and gives a rough-and-tumble talk. The fellows increase their production. Then comes a third secretary and pours out a middle-of-the-road talk. And suddenly, the fellows slow down and start a hidden sabotage. No amount of words makes them work more—After all, what is the plan good for? What do they get out of it?"

In this case, two party functionaries were successful in appealing to the workers to increase production; but here the psychological manipulation reached its limits and could not be carried any further. The third secretary failed in his attempt. The informant was at loss to explain the reasons for the failure, and we can only guess what happened. The strains of the production drive might have evoked the unexpected reaction; or an ill-chosen phrase of the third secretary might have revived a forgotten frustration of the workers. In any case, one point seems to be clear: human manipulation is a subtle affair that cannot be perfectly controlled by the manipulator; it brings results, but the results are likely to fall short of the targets of state planning.

No plan can be carried out without failures and mistakes. But the totalitarian concept of duty does not acknowledge incidental failures: who fails, does so on purpose. The very same philosophy which denies individual freedom in carrying out duties attributes every mistake to the ill-will of the individual. It turns every failure into a legally defined, severely punished crime, sabotage. The saboteur is the most common witch of the Communist demonology and may come in all sizes. The large-scale saboteur may be an important personality in the regime who is suddenly charged with grave crimes, sometimes with fantastic plots. The mass of toilers are accused of small-scale, but continuous sabotage—lateness and absenteeism, wasting time and material, ruining tools and machines, producing rejects, stealing "social property," and neglecting the work norms.

The official list of acts of sabotage reads like a mystery melodrama. But its venomous public charges should lead us neither to underestimate the efficiency of the Communist production system nor to deny the existence of many shortcomings. Some of the faults are incidental and would crop up anywhere; others may be trumped-up charges against more or less innocent people; others, again, should be attributed to red tape and the party's constant interference with work, to poor equipment and want of investment capital, to the workers' lack of motivation to produce better work, and to other conditions of a totalitarian planned economy. But after all those allowances, a great many "acts of sabotage" do represent the workers' protest against the Communist concept of duty. They are committed deliberately, with the intention of obstructing the political system. Whenever a worker takes a piece of pipe home from the plant to repair his plumbing, he demonstrates that his individual superego has prevailed against the one the party has tried to impose. These small-scale demonstrative acts (more about them later) are numerous in the Communist economy. In sum, they weaken the productivity of the Soviet countries, but their trifling proportions do not affect the existence and power of the political system.

II

Besides work days, there must also be red-letter days in the calendar. Human nature requires that the routine of work should be regularly interrupted, that everyday duties should be put aside, and that activities of solemnity and relaxation should take their place. So it happens in every group. The great American rituals engage an ordinarily hard-working nation and offer a rich variety: civic organizations arrange spectacular fireworks on the Fourth of July, churches offer regular services, universities and high schools organize football and commencement exercises, and the citizen may participate in any of them, according to his liking. The great variety of rituals, ranging from the imposing to the silly, adds a special color to American life.

Communism provides just as many rituals (and perhaps more), but with less variety and less freedom. All of its ceremonies are centrally organized by the party state and bear emphatic reference to the Red superego. The result is a ceremonial calendar which is basically totalitarian; it serves the regime, supports the work plan, and asks for the loyal participation of the citizens when this is desired by the regime. It is an integral part of the Soviet system.

The official calendar of Communism contains three types of rituals, appealing to three particular emotions: the orgiastic, the work, and the cathartic rituals. The orgiastic ritual has its type in the Bacchanals and Saturnalia of antiquity. It is the authorized self-liberation from the accepted inhibitions. It throws overboard those rules and norms which govern humdrum everyday life; it gives the elation of being free and unencumbered. Popular as the orgiastic ritual was in antiquity, Christianity fought it persistently and pushed it back among the folk customs that managed to avoid the control of the Church. In modern times, certain political movements revived the orgiastic rituals and developed them into mass demonstrations in which the presence of the mass proved the strength of the movement and filled the individual with orgiastic intoxication. In this form, the orgiastic ritual became useful to Bolshevism.

Communism has never conceded much importance to individual actions. It has been more concerned with moving big, uniform masses in an imposing way, and this preoccupation has created the most spectacular Red rituals. The reader of the newspapers on August 11, 1957, saw reports of three mass meetings held almost simultaneously in the Communist empire—the World Youth Meeting in Moscow, with 32,000 foreign visitors and several hundred thousand participants from the U.S.S.R.; a meeting at Rostock, East Germany, with Mikoyan as its guest speaker and with an audience of 80,000 to 100,000; and a "local" festival in the small Hungarian city of Kisujszállás with 116,000 admission-paying visitors. The numbers are impressive indeed.

The mobilization of hundreds of thousands needs careful planning and thorough preparation. The whole party apparatus takes part in this job—full-time functionaries, rank-and-file members, activists, temporary helpers, volunteers, and conscripts. When the time for the May Day parade comes along, the house and block trustees drive out every resident in their bailiwick, and the shop trustees make sure that the workers carry the assigned posters and banners. The festive march takes place as planned. The managers of the mass demonstrations leave nothing to chance and pay attention to every possible detail. The foreign delegates who arrived at the World Youth Meeting in Moscow received a standard gift parcel, plus two towels and, as somewhat insulting trinkets, a toothbrush and toothpaste. On May Day, beer and sausages are usually given away, causing some free-for-all scenes at the points of distribution.

Such masses of humanity easily become intoxicated with emotions and behave according to the LeBonian laws of psychology. As a matter of fact, it is the duty of the managers of the demonstrations to channel the emotions of the masses in the direction desired by the party. They work systematically to establish the participants' emotional involvement with the superego, and use banners, toothpaste, direct instructions, and even crude force to fill everybody with the desired feelings.

The rituals of work, no Communist inventions either, have a venerable history. Their classical counterpart shows up in the regular sacrifice of the Roman paterfamilias before the *lares* of his home or in the great Ambarvalia of the farming countryside. Christianity made ample use of them, as the patron saints of medieval guilds, with their special masses and processions, exemplify. Similarly, Communism has worked out a well-planned network of simple rituals that have a plain design, fit into the daily routine, and do not disturb the emotional balance of regular life. The ceremonial meetings of the party, trade unions, and mass organizations follow each other so closely that the citizen may have to attend two or three meetings a week. The meetings are somber but carefully arranged. Their agenda is prescribed in written instructions, and the speakers receive a "syllabus" from the appropriate party organization. For example, the monthly "plan meeting" is called to hear the manager's report on production, to discuss the ever-existing bottlenecks, and to make resolutions for the perfect fulfillment of the state plan. It is usually taken up with the speeches of the production manager, the secretary in charge of planning, and the chairman of the union local, while the audience sits in silence.

The success of ceremonial meetings hinges on the emotional involvement of the audience, and work in itself seldom arouses spontaneous enthusiasm. The American trade unions show a great deal of common sense when they restrict ceremonial meetings to a necessary minimum. The Communist ritual, on the other hand, exhorts the worker as often as possible, even at the risk of boredom. Nevertheless, its effect should not be underestimated. It fills the workers with the impression that their work is tremendously important; it assures them that their work is meaningful.

constructive, and almost sacred. Through this assurance, the ceremonies bolster the self-confidence of the worker and give psychological support to state planning as a whole.

Where the other rituals fail, the cathartic ritual steps in. It is able to resolve the psychological strains that naturally emerge during the performance of duties. No duty and no goal can be pursued smoothly. The difficulties that emerge produce strains and tensions in the individual, fill him with doubts about his ability to attain the goals. The strains may be removed by a confession of his shortcomings, an introspective evaluation of his abilities, a strengthening of his decision to pursue his duties. Confession or psychoanalysis offers relief to those who wish to utilize it. Many people achieve their catharsis through a self-criticism performed without any ritual ceremonies. As a matter of fact, self-criticism is a natural part of man's intellectual activity. He scrutinizes his behavior in order to correct his mistakes. In our Western culture this self-criticism is carried out in loneliness or among a small circle of intimates. It is a private affair, undertaken at one's own discretion, carried on without publicity.

Communism, however, has made a public ritual out of self-criticism. The party requires that the members constantly subject themselves to self-criticism—and the rule in itself would not endanger the intimate, non-ceremonial character of the act. In practice, however, self-criticism is non-spontaneous and public. It is channeled; it is directly ordered by the authorities. As an American scholar put it succinctly, "The party itself, through its leading organ—the Central Committee—is the one that provides guidance with regard to the timeliness, propriety, tenor, and extent of complaints and accusations, and the concrete goals sought through self-criticism."[5]

From time to time, selected members are summoned to perform self-criticism before the authorities of the party, before fellow members and co-workers, and, in important cases, before the public press. No freedom is permitted. The member must acknowledge his error and omit the extenuating circumstances; if ordered by the party, he must confess imaginary errors. He must use the ritual words and expressions. He must prostrate himself before the party, deliver himself to its mercy, and expect the catharsis resulting from the ritual forgiveness of the party. Reports from Russia assert that old fighters of the movement who had faced danger, jail, torture, and possible death for the party trembled and shed tears when called on for such performances.[6]

Catharsis is a complex process, ending in a strengthened identification with the superego and strengthened confidence in oneself. The forced cathartic ritual of Communism often achieves this fulfillment. Self-criticism has a great appeal to people whose psychological needs include self-accusation and public self-abasement. In one case with which I became acquainted, the party member gained much satisfaction out of the self-critical denunciation of his bourgeois family background he made before a party control committee. Another party member, one of the faithful, hard-working kind, described self-criticism as a useful and necessary process for the control of the self, for regulating one's work and one's relationship to the superego. He claimed to have used self-criticism constantly as a part of his work routine, being ready for the public ritual at any time. Other informants claimed that self-criticism restored the faith of many who had been overcome with doubt, weakness, and hesitation.

This aspect of self-criticism had a special meaning for the peoples of Russia. Among them (as the great Russian writers as well as Western observers have repeatedly noted) public self-abasement and the acceptance of guilt and guilt feelings were rather common inclinations that were displayed before intimates and strangers alike and approved by the culture of the society.[7] On the other hand, among those seven peoples who were destined to furnish the second generation of Soviet man, a quite different attitude had prevailed. The Czechs, Germans, and Hungarians, following the norms of their native culture in their personal behavior, need a strong ego assertion in public. For them, self-criticism is a public humiliation, a punishment to be abhorred and feared. "I felt," recalled one informant who was purged from the party, "as if I were standing stark naked in the center of a crowd and everybody was poking fun at me." At the time of the party purges, when self-criticism is carried out en masse, the control committees indulge in asking indiscreet questions about sex life, drinking habits, financial affairs, or the social deportment of spouse and children. The result is frequently an alienation from the party rather than a strengthening of faith.

No doubt the Red rituals provoke ambiguous sentiments. Still, they appeal to emotions and may fill the subject with a great amount of gratification and good feeling. They are for many the most popular part of the Red system and offset many of those resentments that are caused by the centrally assigned work duties and strict labor discipline. Orgiastic rituals enhance loyalty, work rituals have propaganda value, and self-criticism helps to maintain discipline. The Red rituals are useful and have an importance equal to that of work itself. They are public and are publicized. The press extensively reports on the daily acts of the liturgy, describing each of them according to its importance. A ritual text, a manifesto or speech, is printed *in toto*; it may cover several pages, more than half of the entire issue of the paper. It makes dull reading to those who do not share the Communist faith, but the Soviet papers are not published for their news value; they are the official mouthpiece of the superego.

In all rites, words have a magic role. Their purpose is not supposed to be the free and sincere expression of the individual. Ceremonies use a ritualistic style, like the sacred style of many religions that follows accepted idioms and metaphors and disregards the requirements of content and communication. The Red superego in all its utterances must speak in a ritual style, putting together nothing but the sacred words and approved ideas. Its writers must use the imagery developed by Lenin and Stalin—for example, the metaphor of fire and water that do not mix. They must frequently use the words "people" and "masses" in the sense that the party understands them. The Communist government is the "people's government," "people's democracy," and "people's republic," and there are a "people's economy" and "people's culture," as if the economy and culture were the reflections of the free will of people. In the history books, the revolution approved by the party is the revolution of the people and the war is the war of the Russian people against the oppressing Ukrainian *hetman* or Polish gentry.

The ritual style is compulsory in newspapers and belles-lettres, in historiography and geography, in art and movies. Newspaper reporter, party theoretician, novelist, artist, all without exception have to speak in the common ritual style. Not even visitors are excepted. The French writer André Gide, touring the U.S.S.R., wanted to send a few words of homage to Stalin; alas, the telegraph office would not accept any other text but the prescribed ritual, and the telegram was never sent.

Repetition is the essence of a ritual style, and the pronouncements that pass Communist censorship are astonishingly alike. They repeat the same ideas, dressed in the same verbal garb. Any touch is suppressed that would add color or originality; humor, that playful manifestation of human shrewdness, was forbidden up to the time of Khrushchev. Through the writers and artists, only the superego can speak, and its voice is as grim and gray as the sky on a November afternoon. Man's natural desire to express himself freely is stifled. The intellectual, whose main profession is self-expression, feels an excruciating frustration, but the less articulate subject may slowly forget how to use his own words and formulate his own ideas.

In any ritual system it is a question of great importance who should be authorized to perform the rites. Many groups appoint a special class, priests for example, to carry out this function. The monolithic Communist system entrusts the performance of rituals to the same people who run the party apparatus and hand down its teachings. The Communist leader has complete authority to explain the superego and initiate rituals. The importance of a leader can be best measured by his part in the rituals. The top-level leader delivers the festive speech, and he also accepts the homage of the subjects. Leaders at the lower levels perform some auxiliary function; they may organize the liturgy, take care of the technical details, and herd the masses out for the celebration.

The top leader officiates at the most important rituals and, in turn, is honored there. His name and picture appear on the banners carried by the masses; he is greeted, applauded, venerated. Although Communist philosophy denies individual leadership and emphasizes Lenin's principle of collective leadership, practice is somewhat different. Any leader, once accepted, becomes the center of a ritual hero worship. As soon as he takes over the party machine, he is elevated to a lofty level. His figure loses all human traits and assumes the improbable qualities of a mythical hero. So it happened with Lenin, whose mythology was built up in the 1920's. Ever since, the official historiography depicts him as the amazing genius whose leadership was immediately recognized by everybody, by his siblings as well as by the peasants in the village of Shushensko in Eastern Siberia where he lived as an exile of the Czarist police. He possessed, so it is claimed, the superhuman ability to give the right answer to every question and was destined to become the founder of the most perfect superego. One of the strange results of the creation of this attractive, mythical image is that Lenin is worshiped by many defected Communists, by refugees, and even by unprejudiced scholars of the Western World. Hero worship appeals everywhere to basic psychological needs, and frequently one's hero is picked by accident rather than by careful consideration.

The Stalin mythology was fabricated in his own lifetime, and from an early period at that. Its beginnings can be traced back to the Fourteenth Congress of the party in 1925, when the applause given to Stalin against the opposition of Kamenev openly acknowledged him as *vozhd,* the leader. Subsequently, he became the "good father" of all subjects, an image adopted obviously from the imperial ritual of Czarism. As an amplification of his fatherly role, he became the "little comrade" of the pioneers; he became a military genius credited with winning not only the civil war but also World War II; he became the best critic and inspiration of the literary world—though he was an image showing strange intellectual traits; he became an expert linguist and an authority in many learned fields.

After Stalin's death, the new leadership of Khrushchev turned against the "personal cult." It remains to be seen whether Communism can survive without hero worship or whether the fight against the personal cult means only a change in the identity of the heroes who are worshiped. At present, Khrushchev emerges as a new mythological hero, not the intellectual-superman type like Lenin, not the fatherly image like Stalin, but the uninhibited, emotional, loquacious, and good-humored type of folk hero, like Taras Bulba or Hadji Murat.

The official propaganda creates myths of superhuman leaders, and then the ritual of hero worship tries to make the myths come true. The rituals, indeed, treat the leader as if he were a superman, basically different from common mortals, as if he were the ever-present, eternal guardian of the superego. The mythical belief in the omnipresence of the leader is well symbolized in the works of such artists as N. Andreev, who has turned out more than a hundred portraits of Lenin under such titles as "Lenin, the Leader." The ritual formula for ending all speeches, "Long live the U.S.S.R.! Long live the party of the working proletariat! Long live our leader Comrade Stalin!," reminds one of the eternal connections between the superego and the leader. The Lenin mausoleum at the walls of the Kremlin, with its daily procession of visitors, recalls the Egyptian-Roman belief that heroes, but not common people, might expect everlasting life—contrary as this belief is to the official materialism.

III

Communism regulates work and ritual with a stern hand and stakes out the duties for all. But man fulfills the duties in his own ways, according to his own measures and abilities. One person exerts the utmost efforts to reach his goals and perform his duties thoroughly; another, with less motivation and less effort, does a poor job. In the mass of humanity two common types of workers can be distinguished: the perfectionist and the competitor. The former is satisfied by nothing but the best performance; the latter evaluates his duties in personal terms and tries to outdo his rivals.

Communism appeals to both types and channels their energies into the direction chosen by the party state. Out of the perfectionist, the regime makes a Stakhanovite (or shock worker or hero of labor), who sets a production record and animates the other workers to do the same. The competitor is deprived of individual goals but may participate in the "socialistic work competition" in which factories and kolkhozes compete to turn out more and better goods. Thus, the natural strivings of the best workers are skillfully put to the use of the regime, and the perfectionist and competitor who abide by the official rules are lavishly rewarded for their achievements.

Reward and punishment are necessary consequences of duty. Any superego that sets up duties has to reward their fulfillment and punish their neglect. The sanctions of Communism are conspicuous and formidable (they will be described in a separate chapter). Some of the rewards, however, should be discussed here, since they illustrate the Communist concept of work and ritual.

The superego rewards the faithful with what is valued most by it. Our capitalistic society is much inclined to distribute financial rewards, but the Communist superego is suspicious of money and the free use of money by the citizens; it prefers to give non-material rewards. Stakhanovites and winners of work competitions do receive higher wages and special premiums of considerable value: better housing, better food, and summer vacations. But self-sacrifice has a central place in the Red superego, and Communism is more generous with non-material rewards of "honor" and praise. "In the U.S.S.R.," says Article 12 of the Stalinist constitution, "work is a duty and a matter of honor for every able-bodied citizen." Because he has regarded his personal honor so highly, the Stakhanovite enjoys a great prestige; he is the usual hero of novels, motion pictures, and plays. As the most conspicuous non-material reward, medals, orders, and citations are lavishly bestowed upon those who best fulfill the duties or, at least, are selected as best fulfilling them by the authorities.

The medals, orders and corresponding titles come in different grades, and their bearers constitute the *Légion d'Honneur* of the Red Napoleons. In Hungary, for example, the Red Banner Merit Order of Work is granted to those individuals who are the real pillars of the system, usually for meritorious party work. Ordinary people engaged in production work may receive the Merit Order (or Medal) of Work, which has three grades; those who excel in competition may get the citation of "Excellent Worker," the miners have their own Service Medal, and the citation "Excellent Master of Trade" is given to small artisans. A Merit Order of Motherhood is granted for production in this area, its first grade being awarded for twelve children. The Medal for Socialistic Culture is the reward of the amateur supporters of cultural affairs, while professional artists, actors, and writers, as well as athletes, have their own decorations, citations, and prizes.

The medals, orders, and titles represent an elaborate hierarchy that is very similar to the hierarchy of the Byzantine or Czarist courts. The lower grades are open to both members of the party and nonmembers; on ritual occasions honors of this kind are showered upon the "good workers." On the Seventh Hungarian Railroad Workers Day, for example, seven workers were decorated with the Merit Order of Work, 28 with the Merit Medal for Socialistic Work, 57 with the Merit Medal of Work, 86 with the Medal of Excellent Railroad Worker, and 204 with the Medal of Meritorious Railroad Worker. Over a period of ten years, Merit Medals alone were given to no less than 1181 railroad workers, and altogether almost 5000 out of the 170,000 railroad workers of the country received some kind of order, medal, or citation.[8] The bemedaled workers, wearing their distinctions on their overalls, make up a conspicuous élite at every parade. Their marching columns prove that Communism, after all, duly rewards fidelity, work, and a sense of duty.

But if an elaborate hierarchy of titles exists, where is that equality of all citizens so often stressed in the Red announcements? Is the Red practice just a publicity stunt the intent of which is to keep those people happy who do not get material rewards? Or is it, indeed, a sign that no equality exists?

V. DEGREES OF PERFECTION

ONE INFORMANT selected the following anecdote to characterize Communism. The peasants of a co-operative were riding to town when their carriage overturned and dumped the passengers into a deep mudhole. Young Andrew, the strong man, struggled hard to free himself, but the more he struggled, the deeper he sank. Suddenly he noticed that he was sinking under the weight of the secretary of the Youth League, who was sitting on his shoulders. "Secretary," he shouted, "why don't you get off my shoulders?" "I can't," was the answer, "because the chairman of the kolkhoz is sitting on my shoulders." "Chairman," shouted Andrew, "why don't you get off the shoulders of the secretary?" "I can't," was the answer, "because the local party secretary is sitting on my shoulders." "Comrade," cried Andrew, "why don't you get off the shoulders of the chairman?" "I can't," was the answer, "because the district party secretary is sitting on my shoulders." And whatever Andrew did, he could not get those people off his shoulders.

The anecdote is old in its motif but illuminating in its application. And indeed, the very political system whose aim is "from each according to his ability, to each according to his needs" has established a conspicuous inequality of men. It divides society into layers, the members of which are sharply distinguished by their power, occupation, privilege, and way of life; it ranks the layers and builds them into an official hierarchy. It justifies glaring inequality with the claim that a more perfect identification must be rewarded with greater recompense and that everybody's place in the hierarchy is the just counterpart of his loyalty. The French

Communist Party tersely formulated the slogan, "Every man in his place, according to his merits, his capacities."[1]

I

The centralized assignment of all duties permits the same central organ to allot every man's place in society, in accordance with his loyalty and devotion. To be sure, Communism demands perfect identification from all, and one may argue, logically, that the adjective "perfect" cannot have gradations. The party, however, makes allowances for human nature and tacitly admits that some comrades are more, others less, devoted. It recognizes more perfect and less perfect people and allots rights and privileges in proportion to the individual's degree of perfection. In fact, it creates more equal and less equal subjects.

The actual inequality is based upon practical considerations. The service of the Red superego needs definite classes of people who do specific jobs. In practice eight classes have come to exist, distinguished by the importance of their work as well as by their material and non-material rewards. The higher a class is, the more privilege and power it enjoys; in particular, it has power to direct all classes below itself. The party evaluates every subject and places him in one of the classes. The citizen receives his job, class, prestige, and status by central assignment and in proportion to his faith. Eight classes make up the social pyramid.

The *upper cadre* is the official name of a small élite at the top of the social pyramid which exercises the highest leadership in the party state.[2] It exercises the "collective leadership" that is destined, in the words of Lenin, to direct the "joint labors" of the masses and to ensure "that the masses unquestioningly obey the single will of the leaders."[3] Its members are not equal among themselves but have differing degrees of personal power; yet they have achieved the highest positions in the Communist system. Their might is limited by the interest of the party and the personal struggle within the cadre but by no other law or outside agency. They are entrusted with a formidable power by virtue of their perfection. For perfect they are. They are mystically unified with the basic norms and values, they are the embodiments of the superego and the paragons for the rest of the population. As Bukharin remarked, "Good leaders are leaders because they best express the proper tendencies of the party."[4] One official declaration called them "the best, most experienced Leninists," and Molotov described them as "worthy pupils of the great Lenin," as "assistants of our teacher," as "worthy of the people."[5]

Is this official image of perfection a pure invention, created to rationalize these elevated positions? Or is it a true picture of those who govern the Soviet empire? According to the evidence given by disillusioned Communists in the Western countries, the leaders are, indeed, better acquainted with the doctrines, more active and more dedicated, less preoccupied with personal emotional problems, and more ruthless, harder, and more cynical.[6] Obviously, the upper cadre is recruited from men whose personalities combine two usually quite incompatible traits—absolute indentification with the party and skill at political maneuvering. This is a rare combination indeed. The absolute devotion to an idea, psychologists usually contend, is associated with rigidity in character; on the other hand, the skillful maneuvering in a personal struggle requires a great flexibility. The member of the upper cadre must be as stern and uncompromising as the Red superego itself; but only that person reaches the upper cadre who has emerged victoriously from the neverceasing struggle among party functionaries, who has shrewdly steered his course in a sea of personal intrigues and has boldly defeated all his rivals.

The leaders are not selected systematically but emerge as victors in the free-for-all fight for power. They have to start as novices of the party, but as they slowly make their way upward and pass through the grades of the hierarchy, they meet many critical tests and have to prove their ability and devotion each time. The practical tests in the rough-and-tumble situations of life sift the chaff from the grain. Many candidates fail, and those few who succeed are devoted believers. Their selection ensures the safety of the system, for a victor in the struggle for power is unlikely to turn into a Napoleon and crush the revolution that elevated him.

The upper-cadre members enjoy special privileges which help them in their arduous tasks and symbolize their status. They receive those luxuries of life which are not available to the toiling masses. They are furnished with secretaries and servants, with the paraphernalia of an appropriate social life, with all the available goods and services. One Communist writer bitterly attacked this system, claiming that the leader "through his car, pay, apartment, special store, resort, etc., was set apart from life, people, and party, raised himself above the people and the party, prostituted himself to maintain his rule over others, became filled with a maddening sense of superiority, and now looks down upon the people."[7] To be sure, the leader in the upper echelon is not a member of the mass and has left the life of the toilers far behind. His privileges, however, are attached to his office and not to his person. A fall from power cuts off all advantages immediately. The cottage must be vacated, the car and chauffeur relinquished for the benefit of the successor.

There are many privileges, but the burdens are just as numerous. Leadership entails hard work. In the managerial class of America as well as in the upper cadre of the Soviet countries, only those people succeed who dedicate themselves entirely to their work. As an additional load, the Communist leader must constantly live up to the image of the "best," to the role of the "perfect," an inhumanly severe requirement for any human being, imperfect by nature. In order to ease this burden, the life of the Red leaders is clouded in a complete secrecy. The very leaders who are supposed to watch everybody are unknown and unseen. They appear before the masses under rare, ritualistic circumstances only and conceal themselves when they perform their crucial work—making policy. Their human personality is hidden before everybody except a few close collaborators. It is a rare case when one of them discards the ritualistic image and tries to reveal his personality to the subjects. The popularity of Imre Nagy in Hungary was greatly due to his efforts to manifest himself and express some of his doubts, an attitude which is usually not permissible.

The upper-cadre man is lonely and unpopular, and this is the usual lot of despots; moreover, he is not spared the greatest of occupational hazards. In no other political movement have so many leaders been killed, sometimes by the Communist party and at other times by the enemies of the party. As the only acceptable proof of their perfection, the leaders must sacrifice their lives whenever doing so may be useful to the party or whenever they lose out in the personal struggle. Trotsky, with great foresight, eulogized them as "a new Communist order of Samurai" who "could die and teach others to die for the cause of the working class."[8] And when death comes for the leader, he must live up to the official image and depart ritually, like a Samurai, asserting to the last his perfect identification. The two leaders of the illegal Communist Party in Hungary, Imre Sallai and Sándor Fürst, on their way to the gallows shouted propaganda slogans and were silenced only by the final pressure of the hangman's noose. Zoltán Schönherz, a third leader of the illegal party, a few minutes before his execution penned orders to continue the organizational work. A fourth one, Endre Ságvári, was caught by the police in a pastry shop among the conversing young couples. He pulled a gun, staged a battle, and, to keep his secrets from the police, killed himself with the last bullet.

The *middle cadre,* holding down the middle-range jobs of party and state administration, is less perfect and has less authority, fewer privileges, and, perhaps, fewer occupational hazards. Members are regarded as the personal disciples of the upper cadre and prepare themselves for the day when eventually they may step into the posts of leadership. The existence of their well-trained and dedicated group is a constant menace and instigation to the leaders of the upper cadre. In times of crisis, the latter are duly warned that the substitutes are ready to take their places: "Those persons high up in the leadership who fail to stand their own ground will be replaced."[9]

It is like a fight among wolves. The middle-cadre threatens the security of the upper-cadre and is itself threatened from below. Anonymity, the usual fate of middle-cadre people, adds to their insecurity. In the years of Stalin, even the appointment of such a high official as a deputy minister was left unmentioned in the press. The middle-cadre people are not important enough to get their names publicized. They are known to the leaders but unknown to the masses. Being known to the leaders is their hope for a successful future; being unknown to the masses makes it easy for them to assume the ritualistic pose when called to leadership.

The *lower cadre,* which carries out minor administrative functions, is present in every factory and village. The masses of ordinary citizens cannot contact the upper cadre and can rarely contact the middle one, but they regularly meet the ubiquitous lower functionaries. The latter cannot be protected by secrecy but have to work and live under the eyes of the citizens. They have to represent the party before the masses and, at the same time, get their job done. The two requirements, when taken together, make up a very difficult task.

"A work style like Lenin's" is demanded from them.[10] This ritual phrase expresses the same idea as the slang which refers to the lower functionaries as "party hacks": theirs is the drudgery of getting a hard job done. The party secretary in one small village was described as working 12 hours a day; another functionary from the industrial sector complained of the "nervous strain" of his job. The lower-level bureaucrats are flooded with instructions, orders, and memoranda that are often beyond their comprehension but that they have to carry out to the complete satisfaction of their superiors.

The member of the lower cadre can resolve his strain and tension through rigid behavior. He sticks to every dot of the official papers and considers the letter but not the spirit of his instructions. This formalism may easily cover his insecurity or lack of real devotion and guarantees the fulfillment of the orders coming from above. With his occupational rigidity, the lower-cadre official resembles the eternal type of the army sergeant. And indeed, many subjects have the impression that in every aspect of their lives they are bossed by a sergeant who keeps the Soviet administration going in a military, rigid, unpopular fashion.

The *activist* is the part-time voluntary helper, so far as there is anything voluntary in the Communist system. He may be a party member or a nonmember and may be active in educational or propaganda work or in any minor function of the trade unions and other mass organizations. The party welcomes the help of such nonmembers as "workers, working peasants, intelligentsia, young men and women who have adopted the policy of the party, who love the party and are willing to fight self-sacrificingly for the realization of the aims of the party."[11] An efficient party secretary is supposed to be able to organize a large number of activists to help him in the various duties of lesser importance and thereby to increase the efficiency of his work.

"The man to whom people listen" is best suited to be an activist,[12] and that qualification makes him comparable to the civic leader in America. The warning is given, however, that the activist should not be "intimidated and ridiculed" but "acknowledged" by his superiors, suggesting that he must be a little fellow under the thumb of a cadre man and must lack the freedom and independence of the American civic leader. Why, then, does the activist accept his arduous role? Perhaps he is an opportunist who desires security and privilege in his job or wishes to use his connections as a steppingstone towards the higher echelons. Perhaps he was at one time a militant member of the trade union movement and accepts a minor office out of dedication not to the party but to the trade union. Finally, perhaps he lacks any personal motive but signs up under more or less pronounced pressure; and if he has not "adopted the policy of the party" and has not "loved the party," he will surely come to do so under the efficient leadership of an energetic party secretary.

The *rank-and-file party members* are officially still put into the group of "the most active and politically most conscious citizens," of "the vanguard of the working people."[13] In reality, however, they constitute the medium range of a hierarchic society. They are raised above the masses without a membership card, but they lack the personal power of the cadre people; they are neither fish nor fowl. This somewhat awkward position entails a twofold duty—towards superiors, the passive duty to obey willingly and learn diligently; and towards inferiors, the active duty to teach, organize, and animate.

The rank-and-file have not yet given sufficient proof of their devoted identification. As their perfection is doubtful, they cannot be left alone to make their individual progress towards the ideals of a good Communist. They must constantly be supervised and taught. They must be made to take a heavy schedule of educational courses and party work. They must put themselves, at any hour of the day, at the disposal of the party and propagate the Red superego: visit neighbors and strangers, "agitate," solicit subscriptions, sell political pamphlets, or carry, in any other useful way, the official teachings to the masses.

The party is the élite guard. It is severely restricted in size, and the *masses* of the subjects stay outside it. Officially they are called "politically less developed comrades" and are not regarded as being perfect enough to be initiated into the esoteric superego. They are supposed to join the "mass organizations"—trade unions, Youth League, etc.—where they are taught that simplified and popular version of the Red lore that is commensurate with their degree of perfection. Easier duties and discipline are imposed upon them than upon party members. They are not required to do party work, only to applaud.

The masses must study the popular lore, partake in rituals, accept the authority of the party, and support its policy with enthusiasm. Having satisfied such minimal requirements, they are free from the party discipline, duties, and meetings. For them, the end of working hours marks the beginning of leisure time, which they can spend with family or friends at hobbies or play. They may enjoy a private life not much disturbed by the interference of the party. Of course, they have to pay for these amenities by renouncing the possibilities of advancement. Barred from the better jobs and all the official positions, they are supposed to stay in the background and play a mute, supporting role, like extras on a movie set.

Although the party wishes to "organize" everybody, a good number of people manage to stay out of the mass organizations, to be *outsiders*. They are unencumbered by the small chores of trade union membership and out of the reach of the uninterrupted propaganda. They may live as if Communism did not exist, cutting to a minimum any contact with the regime and dodging the requirements of identification. Relatively, they achieve the greatest freedom from the pressures of Communism. However, by the very same act of withdrawal, they demonstrate their imperfection, negligence, and lack of devotion—personal faults, scorned by the regime. The dear cost of their freedom is their relegation to the lowest "legal" social level. The outsiders are good for nothing but unskilled labor. They are supposed to serve as the crude manpower of production, as the peasants in a backward agriculture, as the cheap substitutes for expensive machinery, still lacking in Eastern Europe. Their economic usefulness makes the party tolerate their evident lack of identification.

The bottom of the pyramid is occupied by the *enemies of the people* whose enmity has been proved by evidence satisfactory to the party. They have been found harboring in their bosoms other superegos and must take the punishment due the intolerable sin of faithlessness. Consequently, labor camps, prisons, and other punitive institutions are allotted them as their proper dwelling places.

These are the eight classes of the Communist hierarchy, and the party state—being the sole entrepreneur and employer—can place every citizen in one of the classes according to his fidelity and usefulness. These two qualities are to some extent interchangeable. The doctor and engineer, for instance, have special skills and knowledge and are thereby destined to occupy high positions in the state bureaucracy; they may easily be promoted into the middle cadre without formally joining the party. The artist, actor, and musician draw salaries from a state theater or publishing house and can be promoted, or demoted, in the same way as anyone else; a successful novelist will be given some official function in the Writers' Guild and assured of a position somewhere in the cadre.

Positions and promotions are important for the Soviet citizen, since the classes differ from one another not only in the possession of power but also in other, visible traits, such as the medals and orders on the lapel of the jacket. The Red Banner Merit Order of Work signals a position in the middle or upper cadre; the title of Stakhanovite belongs to an activist or party member; whereas the lower grades of decorations, such as the Medals of Work, are given to the masses but not the outsiders. Then again, the grades of the hierarchy are distinguished by what they have in material goods. The Communist state, which controls production and distribution, uses the available goods to reward devotion, giving more to the perfect people and less to the imperfect. In Hungary in 1956, for example, cars, refrigerators, and TV-sets were for the exclusive use of people on the cadre level; the activists, party members, masses, and outsiders were visibly separated by the quality of their apartments, furniture, clothing, and vacation trips. Any sharp-eyed observer of social life could easily name many further and still significant differences. As the novelist had it, the party member could afford the luxury of keeping a pet dog in the city but not the outsider.[14]

Social differences, of course, do exist everywhere, but the Communist state planning stiffens rather than softens the partitions between classes. Each resort and hotel is designed for one class, and those facilities open to cadre people are not open to workers, let alone peasants. Special stores, inaccessible to the general public, cater to the officials of the regime. At certain restaurants tipping does exist, and certain theatres and concert halls arrange "protocol performances" for which no tickets are sold to ordinary citizens and the invited official guests are seated in the order of their rank.[15] One of our informants, a white-collar worker on the mass level, never had any dealings with his next-door neighbor, a middle-cadre official. As another informant pointed out, the managers and functionaries used the factory cafeteria at different hours from the workers. Evidently, each class leads a life of its own, a life molded for the service of the party state.

II

The Soviet man, so the official philosophy claims, may become more perfect through his own efforts and may, accordingly, advance in the hierarchy; he may advance, however low his beginnings have been, even to the highest ranks. The degree of perfection, of course, is judged by the party state. It maintains a huge personnel department (called "cadre department" in the official parlance) that watches and evaluates the citizens, rewards some and punishes others, and thus determines the fate of the individual.

How does the cadre department evaluate millions of subjects? Loyalty to a superego can be measured through sophisticated tests familiar in the practice of American psychology. The Red system, however, taboos this kind of testing, frowns upon objective criteria. It relies, instead, upon the judgment of the ranking party members who run the cadre department; in other words, everybody is judged by the more perfect comrades, by the superiors in the hierarchy. Such judges evaluate people mainly on the basis of external and often superficial signs, such as their utility in work and ritual. This particular criterion works well in the case of an engineer or actor; but the average citizen lacks conspicuous utility and must prove his perfection laboriously. If he desires to be promoted, he has to convince the cadre department of his loyalty. It is another question, of course, whether those who pass judgment will take notice of the proofs submitted and evaluate them correctly. After all, the hard work of an underling is not always sufficiently appreciated by the superior. An able worker may fail from no fault of his own, he may even fail because of the negligence of his superior. An extrovert may easily convince his superior with glib talk and advance rapidly, whereas an introvert may fall short in this attempt, however perfect his devotion may be.

A general danger therefore exists that the cadre department will overlook many loyal subjects but promote the climbers, opportunists, adventurers, and others who feign loyalty. The party leadership is sophisticated enough to anticipate this danger and counters it with a disciplinary system that is designed to correct automatically the errors of the cadre.

Communist society is regulated by a strict discipline, administered for ordinary citizens by court and police and for party members by the control and disciplinary committees. Its characteristic feature is the never-allayed suspicion entertained by the authorities about everybody. It is the Oriental type of suspicion, the consequence of secrecy and deviousness. The authorities are wary that more error and faithlessness may exist than are reported to them, and they endeavor to ferret out the hidden cases. Consequently, proof of error is not necessary to incur disciplinary action. From time to time single members or all the members at once are called upon to account for their deportment; they are inspected, re-examined, and judged. This revision of the membership is called a "regrouping of the cadres" in Communist speech, but we call it a "purge." It is a relevant part of the Soviet system, a built-in safety valve that secures the adequate functioning of the mechanism under great pressure.

Its procedure is simple enough. The victim is accused not so much of a concrete error or guilt but of insufficient identification with the regime—and who could defend himself against this charge? An unblemished past is no exoneration, since one can deny his loyalty overnight. Who was faithful yesterday may become an enemy today. Trotsky did more than anybody else to put Communism into power, but his achievements were not the grounds of his acquittal; on the contrary, his very achievements were twisted into a demonic plot against the party. Purges were carried out with the aim of reducing the number of white-collar people, peasants, Jews, and university graduates in the party. Since the official policy changes frequently, anybody may fall into error in spite of himself. An orthodox view expressed today may become an evil deviation by tomorrow. The act of duty carried out conscientiously today may turn into a ghastly crime by next week. An intrigue, when unsuccessful, may be one's own crime; when successful, it may be the evidence of a rival's guilt.

The purges cannot be understood in terms of the legal concepts of the West. When identification is measured, concrete evidence is useless because the guilt is defined in theological rather than in juridical terms. Rykov, the former chairman of the Council of People's Commissars, spelled out clearly the plight of the accused: "Salvation lies only in laying down their arms. Their only salvation, their only escape lies in helping the party to expose and liquidate the remnants, the dregs of the counter-revolutionary organization."[17] As a lesser authority, one of our informants, explained the logic of purges, "Let's suppose that the committee accuses somebody of embezzlement. The clever thing to do is to accept the punishment immediately. In this case, the fellow will be expelled from the party, jailed for a few months, and eventually may be reinstated in the party and in his job. But if he tries to stick to his guns, he will rot in jail for life. One cannot beat the party."

At this point, the logic of the Red superego reaches its most perverse self-contradiction. Identification can be proved only by agreeing completely with the party. If anybody, justly or unjustly, is accused by the authorities, he has to accuse himself as his only defense. During the purges, the defendant often takes over the role of the prosecuting attorney and incriminates himself in crimes he never committed. He does even more. He loyally identifies himself with the party leadership, with the very persons who charge him. He praises those who persecute him and accepts their judgment with a servile gratitude.

The party member must devotedly collaborate with the party even when the work to be done means his own destruction. So many of the best leaders of Communism have done. Zinoviev and Kamenev recanted several times and finally confessed their moral responsibility for the murder of Kirov. Bukharin confessed at his trial, "I consider myself responsible for a grave and monstrous crime against the socialist fatherland and the whole international proletariat." Said Rykov: "I have betrayed my country." The former chief of the GPU, Yagoda, was more profuse. "The fact that I and my fellow-accused are here in the dock and answering for what we have done, is the victory of the Soviet people over counter-revolution."[18] Thus, a great many people, some of them loyal and others not, suffer expulsion from the party, reduction in rank, imprisonment, and, also, loss of life. These are the risks of the practical testing system of the Soviet, and they must be taken by everybody. "Don't praise my courage," exclaimed the Communist poet, "dread lives in my heart."[19] A poet, of course, is supposed to be sensitive and timid. The average party member seems to accept his insecurity with that mixture of courage and dread that permits him to face daily life.

The really strange feature of the disciplinary system is that, at certain times, this Oriental cruelty reverses itself and gives way to the leniency of recruitment campaigns. Having expelled many, the party lowers the barriers of admission and accepts thousands of new members. In Russia, the first purge in 1921 expelled almost one-third of the members, and the great purges in the 1930's reduced membership by almost one-half. In between, however, mass membership drives took place, in 1924, 1927, and 1930, and the biggest one, beginning in 1938, lasted all during the war. In Hungary, the formerly illegal Communist Party came into the open in 1945 and soon initiated a long-range recruiting drive. In the first four months of 1948, 200,000 new members joined the party, that is, more than 2 per cent of the entire population of the country. Then, before the end of the same year, a purge was launched which expelled about one-fourth and demoted an additional one-sixth of the total membership. A second recruiting campaign was carried out in 1952-53, followed by a slow, mild purge. In the revolution of 1956, about half of the members "left" the party voluntarily, the loyalty of the rest was re-examined, and the party was reduced to one-fourth of its former size. After reorganization, a new recruiting campaign was announced in the spring of 1957.

The waves of purges and recruitments produce not only an amazing turnover in the membership but also mass promotions and demotions within the ranks. Those who have been purged may subsequently be readmitted and advanced in the cadres, and those who have been demoted do not lose their chance for promotion. Entrance to the party is like a huge revolving door through which crowds are continuously streaming in and out. This inconsistent and senseless scheme, this gross mismanagement of manpower is, however, a natural consequence of the intra-party struggle and is another part of the Oriental heritage. Similar purges and recruitments occurred in the history of the Turkish Janizaries, the Czarist élite guards, and other strong-arm corps of Oriental despots. These purges are a disaster, and the citizen of a Communist country is helpless against them.

But the farmer returns to his field after a hailstorm, and the Soviet man returns to his trade under similar circumstances, hoping that next time he will fare better. And indeed, this hope is not entirely unfounded.

The social classes of Communism keep the door open, or at least ajar, both for those who come and those who leave. And as the Red system punishes the erring subject by casting him into a lower class and rewards the faithful one by lifting him into a higher one, a great many people move up and down the social ladder. The result is a social mobility which is amazing even to an American observer used to stories of skid-row to success. In the Communist empire every position seems to be temporary. It is just as easy, or difficult, to slip down from a high position as to climb up to it. The life histories of the citizens reveal astonishing cycles of failure and success. Within a short time, any individual may pass from one extreme end of the social hierarchy to the other. The distance from an office of leadership to jail is short indeed, and the disgraceful fall of many Communist leaders can be compared only to the fate of satraps, pashas, and other favorites of Oriental despotism. The fantastic careers of Trotsky, Beria, and Malenkov repeat themselves again and again. The Hungarian János Kádár, a poverty-stricken and dissatisfied laborer in the pre-Communist regime, worked himself into the second-ranking job of the party, was then purged and imprisoned, and was released three years later, only to climb again, this time to the highest job in the country.

The lower levels of society partake of the same mobility. People change their domicile, occupation, and position in rapid succession. The young man who joins the party soon finds himself in an important cadre job and the old cadre official is suddenly demoted; the worker is advanced to a managerial position or the manager transferred into another branch of the industry; the factory worker is ordered into a mine or the clerk in the civil service shifted into the police force. Kolkhoz workers migrate to the city and take factory jobs; then the trend reverses itself, and urban workers flood the rural areas in seach of agricultural employment. This gigantic roller-coaster of life thrills even the on-looker. One Russian folk song reflects the amazement of the spectator:

> Formerly he was a workman,
> He used to sweep away the snow from the
> entrance.
> Now he is chairman
> Of the village district council.

Another folk song mixes the amazement with warning:

> A commissar became Fadey,
> The wealthy man in the village,
> But he did not long adorn his post—
> He fell into the hands of the special police.[20]

In this general mobility, any person may achieve success but not security. Nobody expects to end his life on the level of his success. The possibility of demotion threatens everybody. Society offers few cushions against the jolts and jars of life, few refuges for the social weaklings. Life is unstable, tumultuous, and brutal. Success awaits only those who step over the bodies of their victims.

America, a country of classic social mobility, has huge masses vying for success. But in her free system everybody can compete on his own terms and with rivals selected by him. He can employ his self-selected means to get ahead—hard work, expert knowledge, ruse, influence, intrigue. Success, although not always a logical result of abilities and work, is decided on the level of the rivalry, without the interference of outside agencies such as state and police.

Any success, once achieved, is generally acknowledged and gives a certain security against future vicissitudes.

The Communist system does not tolerate a free struggle and does not tolerate any accumulation of capital. It approves and encourages, however, a keen competition for higher standards of living, personal privilege, and power. "As we demote members," declared the French Communist Party, "who show themselves incapable of performing their tasks, we will be advancing a multitude of young people who display more initiative and enthusiasm. . . . There are responsibilities for every comrade. We have posts commensurate with every level of talent."[21] The party prompts and directs the ambitions into its own channels. The result is a society which is competitive in Communist terms, in which the only way to satisfy one's ambitions is to join the party and advance in the hierarchy. If the youngster desires a car, the Ph.D. acknowledgement, the factory worker a softer job, they all have to turn toward the sole wellspring of success. They have to compete by vying for the favor of their superiors and by denouncing their rivals.

Communist competition in its fury has assumed the character of a Darwinian struggle. Everybody fights for himself, and the stronger eats the weaker. Shelter is hard to find unless one withdraws from the competition and, retiring into a peaceful grove of his own, gives up ambitions. As a matter of fact, every society has its non-competitive members who prefer peace, security, or the pleasure of the hour to the goals of success. In the Soviet countries the two most populous classes, the outsiders and the masses, manage to keep out of the struggle or, at least, to reduce their part in it to a minimum. Perhaps not more than one out of every six subjects is drawn into the whirling maelstrom of success and failure.

Whatever the number, many are those who fail in their ambitions. What happens to them and to their loyalty?

Do they become malevolent and aggressive, or do they make a compromise with the source of their frustration? At this point one has to remember Freud's famous theory: the child is ambivalent towards his father, because he is dependent on him for love and protection but also fears his wrath. Similarly, the Soviet man is dependent on the party state for care and protection but also fears its all-powerful wrath. The child manages to solve his problem: he internalizes the commands and prohibitions of the father and makes the fatherly image into his own superego. Similarly, the Soviet man is supposed to internalize the commands of the party state and make the collective superego a part of himself. As a matter of fact, the regime takes good care that everybody incorporates the prescribed values and goals. This is the essential part of making Soviet men and a main concern of the Communist regime.

VI. CUSTOMS SUBDUED

This story in my collection is about a simple and perhaps hard-drinking janitor of an office building whose main duty was to keep the furnace running and the washrooms clean. In earlier times, when a big bank occupied the office, the janitor did his duty, but he did not care about the company or about the employees, except the managers. In his own way, he liked the managers. He took great pleasure in loitering every morning around the entrance, and when, shortly after nine o'clock, the managers walked in, he would doff his cap and greet them with a humble "Good morning, my Dignified Lords!" Then Communism triumphed and nationalized the bank. The clerks and managers disappeared, and the party moved one of its offices into the building. The janitor suspiciously watched the new clerks taking possession of the old rooms and disliked the newcomers. Soon, however, he came to like the ranking party functionaries and resumed his habit of waiting for them at the entrance. As they walked in, he would doff his cap and say, "Good morning, comrade secretary." And on those occasions when a cabinet minister arrived in the building, our janitor would bow deeply and greet him with a happy smile: "Good morning, comrade minister."

The janitor of our story was equally indifferent towards the theory of the party and the economics of the bank; probably he disapproved of both. But his small job gave him a place in the hierarchy of capitalistic business and, equally, of Communist bureaucracy. With the silly habit of greeting the people at the top, he paid homage to the existing social order and, within it, to his tiny but secure position. The existing order changed, but his habit of acknowledging the people at the top remained the same. He did not feel bound to the norms of a superego but to its human representatives. For some reason and in some way, he internalized the figures of authority and paid equal homage to the executives of the bank and to those of the party. That was enough. He found a place for himself within the system, accepted the existing order, and performed a modest and yet meaningful function.

It is always through a subtle and nonconscious process that people accept common goals and values. Nevertheless, human groups and organizations aim for a strong solidarity and cannot rely on chance. They try in many ways to enforce their values and work hard for this aim. They cannot absolutely ensure the desired result, but they constantly influence their members to internalize the collective superego. They have developed three main ways of exerting that influence: custom, persuasion, and command.

Customs, folkways, mores, traditions, are the accepted ways of doing things. They represent spontaneous agreements, based upon a consensus and followed through time-honored usage. In small and simple communities consensus is easily reached, and customs regulate all the daily activities: farming and family life, government and competition, social intercourse and religious practice. Those who keep the traditions earn public praise; those who break them are disavowed by the community. Although praise and disavowal are efficient sanctions, custom is limited in its efficacy. If the group grows too big and human inter-relations become too complicated, the consensus weakens and cannot support the customs any more. As our mass industrial and urban society developed, many old folkways faded away, and the surviving ones retired into the intimate, private sphere of life. Our society still observes customs in courtship, marriage, social intercourse, and religious practice, but it is mainly influenced by command and persuasion.

Command presupposes the inequality of humans. Commands can be given and obeyed only when some members are subordinated to others. The commander is set above the others by his personal power to enforce his orders, and the subordinates have to obey or suffer punishment. Punitive institutions are as ancient as social inequality, but as our mass society outgrew customs, it had to build more jails to maintain order. Once custom itself policed the townships of New England, but now we need organized police forces to watch our cities.

Persuasion is the rational form of exerting influence, and it appeals to man's reason. It presupposes a free choice between two or more possibilities, as, for example, the choice of picking one out of several available superegos or one out of several commodities on the market. Persuasion induces man to select one possibility and reject the others. It points out the advantages of one possibility and describes it as "better," "more valuable," or "right." Command uses force; persuasion, argument. Its sole sanction is the argument that a good choice will bring advantageous results, further one's own interest, and ensure satisfaction. This is a weak sanction that has restricted the wide use of persuasion. But our era invented the media of mass communication, which can carry the messages of persuasion to all places and people. With this reinforcement, persuasion is rapidly gaining importance and appears as a main force influencing our society.

The leaders of every group wish to achieve solidarity and a common devotion to the superego among the members of the group. Their success in doing so, however, depends on their skill in mobilizing the three available methods of influencing people. Communism has a totalitarian skill in this respect and created an extremely powerful—almost omnipotent—institution to enforce the Red superego. This institution is the party state, which manipulates custom, command, and persuasion and uses them to make loyal Soviet men out of all subjects.

When Communism seized power, it found many vigorous folkways, time-honored usages which survived from the feudal or bourgeois past and aroused the hatred of the new men of power. At first, Communism endeavored to eradicate these usages. Thus came the decade of Mme. Kollontai with her emancipation of women and love, of Yaroslavsky with his League of Militant Atheists, of Lunacharsky, Bukharin, and many other iconoclasts. Communism destroyed the old and partly communal forms of land ownership because of their feudal origin, destroyed many customs of courtship and marriage because of their bourgeois ideals, and destroyed many traditions of religious life because of their conspicuous reference to a non-Communist superego.

As Stalin set out to consolidate his regime, the fight against old customs took a sharp turn. His policy recognized the use of customs, provided the customs could be subdued and refashioned into manageable tools of the party. His aim was that the party should appear as the institution welded together with folkways, with the right and accepted ways of doing things. Thus, Stalin himself emphasized the "folkish" elements of Communism and pictured the party as the protector of the folk and defender of the customs against the enemies of the people.

The policy of consolidation revived many old customs, not in their original forms, but in new guises that were adapted to Bolshevik uses. It introduced customs by administrative order and imposed "pseudo-folkish" traditions upon the people. Old traditions of communal landholding suddenly became useful in popularizing kolkhoz farming and promoting a collectivistic spirit among the peasantry.

Schoolbooks, newspapers, novels, and films extolled "work-bees" and other customary forms of voluntary collective labor. Peasants, laborers, and office workers were supposed to turn out as a body under the banner of the party to build a school or clear a road. The authorities benevolently supported the revival of folk costumes, folk dances, even the somewhat spurious traditions of gypsy music, and managed to smuggle some propaganda into them. They revived an interest in the "old musical instruments of the folk" in order to counteract the popularity of American jazz; they made the "valedictorian week" of the graduating students more elaborate and furnished official speakers who repeated the current slogans of the party. In Hungary (one story tells us) the peasants of the Rákóczi co-operative heard so much talk of traditions that they looked far and near to find a genuine local custom. Since they could not find any other, they ended up by holding a sheep-goulash dinner, promoting therewith the collectivistic spirit.[1]

In every country, colorful folkways center around the feasts of the church. They mark the recurring seasons of the year and designate the times for work and recreation, for festive gatherings and merriment, for public and personal undertakings. Communism rewrote the calendar, wanting nothing less than to replace the old cycle of the year with a party-fashioned one. It hoped that in this way the devotion to the feasts would be transferred to the party.

Its endeavor met some success. The important religious holidays could not be absorbed in the Red ritual, but some party feasts gained popularity. As one informant put it, "When the Communists try to turn Christmas into a Feast of Father Winter, everybody curses them; but when the folk festival of May Day comes, many people like it." The traditional Christmas and Easter could not be replaced with party-inspired rituals; the Feast of Bread partially replaced an old folk holiday, and Labor Day, as a pure party festivity, obtained the limited approval of the masses. Similarly, a number of specifically local festivals were often successfully transformed into well-organized provincial Communist demonstrations.[2]

Religion and social life have established special customs to celebrate those important occasions—birth, coming of age, marriage, death—when a person passes from one stage of existence to another. These customs of passage have been memorable feasts of family life from ancient times, but Communism, in its totalitarian greediness, tried to snatch them from the family circle and attach them to the party. The regime repeatedly attempted to introduce party-centered "baptisms," weddings, and burials, but the population stuck to the old ways.

The "Communist festivity of naming," as the equivalent of baptism is called, takes place at a House of Culture of the Trade Unions, in a festive room decorated with red carpets, flowers, and a reception line of little Pioneers. The elaborate ceremony features a well-selected musical program, recitals by grade-school children, an address by a party functionary, and the official act of the state birth registrar; at the end of the ceremony, each infant is presented with a red necktie, the badge of the Pioneers. The ceremony, which shows the Communist preoccupation with ritual at its best, seems to attract only those families that have chosen the Communist way of life. The great majority of the parents favor the old custom of baptism at a church.[3]

The party-style weddings and funerals appear to be even less popular, but the Youth League, an obliging stooge in these matters, made its initiation ceremony obligatory for all young people, and the youth now celebrates the coming of age in the official fashion. As a matter of fact, the wish of the authorities is to subject the intimate spheres of private life to political authority. The exemplary family calls upon the local council, an administrative unit of the party state, even to straighten out quarrels between husband and wife.[4]

When Communism rose to power, folk art still flourished in the villages of Eastern Europe. The poor peasantry spun yarns, as well as richly embroidering linen, combining thus an economic necessity and a pleasant amusement. Soon Communism interfered. Under the guise of benevolent protector, it organized folk art with that maddening systematism which alone was enough to kill off the freedom of expression. It herded the producers of the famous folk textiles into Home Craft Co-operatives and put them under the supervision of local councils and party units. Almost a thousand women from sixteen to seventy years of age work in the Matyó Home Craft Co-operative in Hungary and produce their folk art under the direction of twenty-seven professional designers.[5]

The regime rewarded folk artists with a monthly salary, the "creative fee," and with the titles of Worthy Folk Artist and Master of Folk Art. In return it asked just one favor—that folk art should speak the language of the superego. The state-supported folk artist could not resist this demand. Now the folk embroidery displays the hammer and sickle and homespun shines with a familiar red color. The teller of folk tales spins his yarn around Red heroes and tells the fable of the poor boy whom capitalism exploited but whom Communism saved by making him a self-conscious proletarian and factory manager.[6] The folk poet, of course, sings of the party as did that unknown partisan of the Russian civil war who composed this poem:

> Through the Sedinsky forests and valleys
> Passed the partisan detachment.
> They marched, they fought for freedom,
> The working people came to help them.
> The bourgeoisie began to wish to drink their fill
> Of the blood of the proletarian workers,

But the bourgeoisie will have to perish
At the mighty hand of the working class.[7]

One may wonder how spontaneous were the feelings expressed in this piece of poetry, which, by the way, was printed and distributed by the Red Army. One may ask how spontaneously those students act who volunteer for summer work in mines, those village girls who decorate the main square for the May Day parade, those workers who overfulfill the quotas of the production plan? Yet, the students, girls, and workers perform these exertions year after year and, as the officials claim, out of custom. Customs, once harnessed, lose their unbidden character and become handmaids to whatever power to which they may be enthralled.

The old customs survived mainly in the countryside, and their manipulation by the party state meant the re-education of the peasantry, this numerous, conservative, and backward social class in Eastern Europe. The regime wanted to liquidate the "stupid, vicious, anti-humanistic, and anti-progressive customs and rules" of the peasantry and did much to eradicate those many superstitions which were contrary to modern standards of public health and social welfare. Yet at the same time, it combined these efforts with its foremost concern—producing Soviet men. Its propaganda repeatedly described individual ownership of the land as the cause of widespread tuberculosis and high infant-mortality and praised Kolkhoz farming as the bright roadway leading to sanitary living conditions and improved health care.[8] And the peasant woman, who nowadays is more likely than not to bear her baby in an obstetrical ward, has at least one good reason to appreciate the advantages that the new ways offer her.

The same political movement that manufactured an all-pervasive superego tried to build up a Communist way of life as the pattern of existence for the good and faithful citizen. It takes, however, more time and more social stability to develop customs than to make up an ideology. The forty-odd years of Communist rule in Russia and its much shorter life in the satellite countries have been too brief a period to establish a consensus among the population. In consequence, not so much custom but rather the other forms of influence enforce the Red superego. One is the daily persuasion of the official propaganda, and another is the daily terror of the official commands—two essential characteristics of Communism that will be investigated in the following chapters.

VII. PROPAGANDA AS A MONOPOLY

The party secretary in a small city (so goes the story) received a very important assignment: to organize an exhibition on germ warfare. He toiled for days, spruced up the local House of Culture and carefully arranged the exhibition material sent down from party headquarters. He displayed pictures, shell-casings, newspaper clippings, and testimonials to prove that the Americans had waged germ warfare against the peaceful citizens of Korea. The most priceless item, an infected flea, was supposed to be put under a huge magnifying glass in the center of the House of Culture. It was a specimen too precious to be left out for the night, and the secretary took it home with him. The next morning, however, when he was ready to leave for the solemn opening of the exhibition, he could not find the flea. He searched through his whole apartment, looked into every corner and drawer, but in vain. He had lost the priceless flea that could best have proved the charges of the party. Having committed such a grave breach of faith, he dared not show up at the House of Culture. Instead, he fled into the woods and wandered restlessly until, utterly exhausted, he fell asleep under a tree. Frightening dreams visited him even then. He saw the party as a giant flea the size of a mountain, holding scores of people in its infected jaws. He tried to do his duty and catch the flea, but whenever he came close, the monster jumped and was miles away again. He could not reach it, the party eluded him all the time. . . . When he awoke in the moonlight, his body was still perspiring from the imaginary hunt. And still haunted by fear and remorse, he climbed a tree and crept out on a strong branch. There he removed his suspenders, wrapped them around his neck, fastened their ends to the branch, and dropped silently into the dark air. Two days later some lumbermen found his body dangling from the branches and dancing in the wind.

Into the macabre story of the little party secretary can be read the protest of an angry intellectual against the unending Communist propaganda. The propaganda is futile, says the intellectual, and many Western commentators agree with him. The Red leaders, on the other hand, regard it as effective and fruitful, and they must have some knowledge on this point.

Persuasion is ancient in its origin, and Socrates of Athens was not the first man who made regular use of it. Socrates' persuasion, however, was restricted to a narrow circle of friends, and the power of persuasion remained weak until the dawn of modern times. Then Western civilization discovered reason and required that man should act reasonably and seek helpful advice. The rise of democracy restrained the exercise of personal power, emphasized the will of the majority, put importaant issues to the vote, and created a new need for persuasion. In time, our advancing technology presented us with marvelous inventions—motion pictures, radio, television—which increased the potential of persuasion almost beyond limits. Now the media of mass communication carry the messages of persuasion everywhere. Everybody can be addressed. Space and time pose no limits.

America, with her rationalistic ideals, democratic institutions, and highly developed system of mass communication, uses persuasion on an impressive scale; advertising, publicity, and propaganda are characteristic features of her daily life. The Soviet countries, with their unlimited state power and incessant pursuit of the superego, avail themselves just as eagerly of the media of persuasion. Although engaged in the same general persuasive activities, the two systems go about them in sharply different ways:

Democratic	*Communist*
a) Freedom of media. The citizenry at large is free to use the available media of communication.	a) Monopoly of media. Only the party state and its appointed spokesmen are permitted to engage in propaganda. Private messages are suppressed.
b) Freedom of content. All messages, even competing ones, can be advertised. Any manufacturer is free to claim that his product is the best and to employ his own arguments and experts to support the claim.	b) Monopoly of content. Only the ideas of the official superego can be propagandized. Contradictory or neutral opinions are silenced.
c) Freedom of belief. Every listener is free to criticize and, for reasons of his own, to accept or reject the persuasion. Nobody can be forced to believe a message.	c) Obligatory belief. Every message of the superego must immediately be accepted. Incredulity is not permitted.
d) Commercial character. Mass persuasion is carried out by private enterprises for their own profit, and media are bought and sold on the open market.	d) Political character. All media are controlled by the party state and operated for its exclusive benefit.
e) Private character. Persuasion is a private affair. Business advertising and political propaganda are clearly separated. The state power and civic organizations do not interfere with political propaganda.	e) Totalitarian character. All citizens, civic and social organizations, and the entire state administration must be active in propaganda and fully support its aims.

The art and labor that America puts into her advertising business are used by the Communists in their official propaganda; nor has the party state any function more important than the over-all enforcement of the superego. Propaganda takes precedence over administration and production and consumes a good part of the Communist society's money, effort, and creative spirit. "Every sacrifice must be made," declared Lenin, "the greatest obstacles must be overcome, in order to carry on agitation and propaganda systematically, perseveringly, persistently, and patiently."[1]

The masses must be permeated with the Red philosophy, and this dynamic goal requires that persuasion should never falter. To this end, the Communist state maintains a tremendous organization which keeps the flow of propaganda continuously moving from the highest levels of the party down to the lowest levels of the citizenry. The flow of the official persuasion is directed by the leaders in the upper cadre, who plan the propaganda much the same way as they plan industrial production and state administration. As Stalin bluntly put it, "In order to overcome difficulties and achieve success, the mobilization of the masses of the workers and peasants to fight for the application of the slogans and decisions of the party and of the government" is an absolute necessity.[2]

As a part of the general policy, the leaders map out the propaganda campaign, which is then carried out by the Central Agitation and Propaganda Department of the party. The Agitprop (as it is called in the parlance, although its official name and competence have changed several times) takes charge of the practical details, issues instructions to the subordinate organs and co-ordinates the nation-wide activities. It controls an enormous apparatus that is supposed to reach all the subjects. It uses all possible media and organizations in spreading the message of the party. It

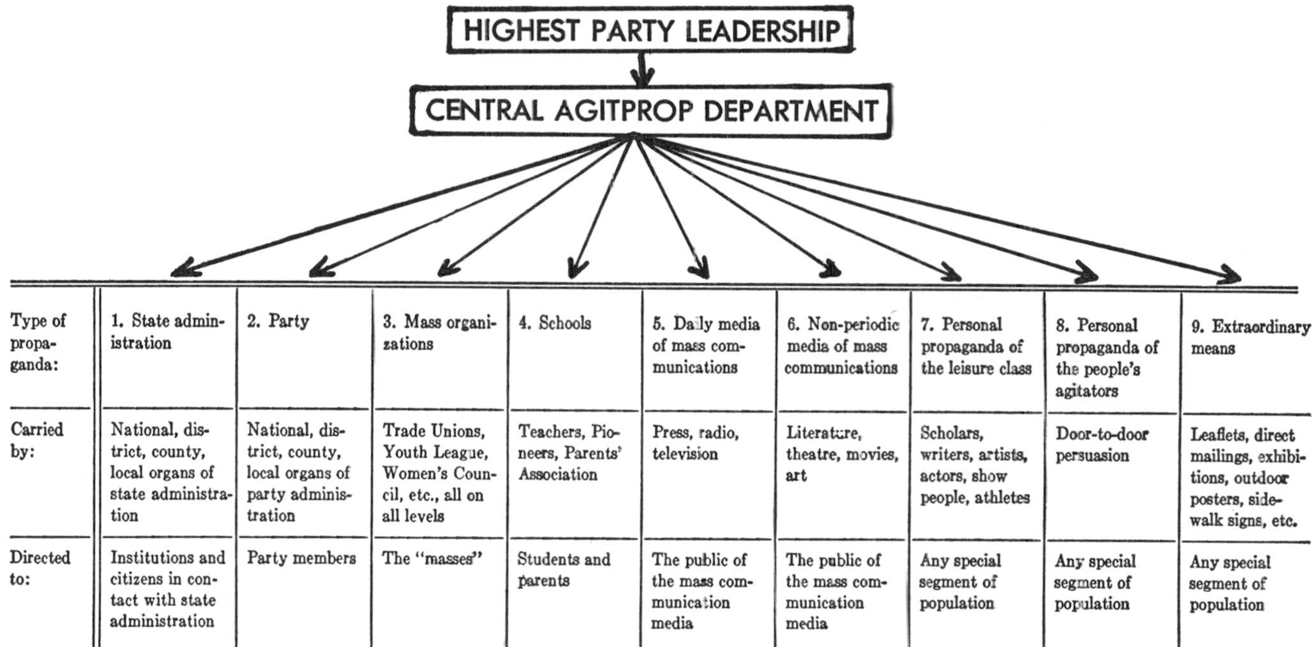

Type of propaganda:	1. State administration	2. Party	3. Mass organizations	4. Schools	5. Daily media of mass communications	6. Non-periodic media of mass communications	7. Personal propaganda of the leisure class	8. Personal propaganda of the people's agitators	9. Extraordinary means
Carried by:	National, district, county, local organs of state administration	National, district, county, local organs of party administration	Trade Unions, Youth League, Women's Council, etc., all on all levels	Teachers, Pioneers, Parents' Association	Press, radio, television	Literature, theatre, movies, art	Scholars, writers, artists, actors, show people, athletes	Door-to-door persuasion	Leaflets, direct mailings, exhibitions, outdoor posters, sidewalk signs, etc.
Directed to:	Institutions and citizens in contact with state administration	Party members	The "masses"	Students and parents	The public of the mass communication media	The public of the mass communication media	Any special segment of population	Any special segment of population	Any special segment of population

Fig. 1. The Totalitarian Flow of Propaganda in a Communist State

operates through nine main lines, which are enumerated in Figure 1.

Each element of the propaganda machine has some special function. The state administration (following the old formula of Potemkin) takes care that reality is adjusted to the requirements of the propaganda, that, for example, saboteurs and foreign agents are arrested and the production targets are reached whenever the slogans demand these things. The meetings of the party and mass organizations repeat the propaganda slogans, make resolutions, and offer voluntary labor, and so do the schools on a junior level. The press, radio, television, being popular and effective vehicles of ideas, carry the messages in subtly disguised, entertaining forms, and so do poetry, novels, movies, stage plays, and art. Creative talents create propaganda and nothing else. "Go, poem, and be a fighter of the class struggle!" exclaimed one of the great poets,[3] and Khrushchev demanded that writers show a greater interest in the urgent tasks of the party, such as the project for the development of virgin lands and the decentralization of industry.[4]

The regime gets what it wants: propaganda material from artists, actors, writers. It gets the same from people in all other walks of life. The Red gentlemen of leisure, the outstanding scholars, sportsmen, and show people, receive privileges, titles, an easy life, but in return they have to endorse every action of the party, sign manifestoes, issue press statements, and deliver speeches. The common men are organized as "people's agitators" on a grandiose scale. Before the election of 1949, the Hungarian Communist Party mobilized 250,000 people's agitators, who visited and propagandized every voter at least twice.[5] And it is impossible to cite all the extemporized means used by mass propaganda. Advertising in America has devised an amazing variety of media—balloons and blotting papers, match boxes and ball-point pens, outdoor signs and sky-writing—to carry the messages of persuasion. Communism has been just as ingenious in procuring its own media: wall newspapers, posted at every factory, office, and school; direct mailings, sent out by factories and mass organizations; road companies and puppet theatres, touring the remote countryside. An extreme example, perhaps, but even horse racing is utilized, the horses being named after mines, factories, and other glorious marks of Communist achievement.

Upon receiving orders, the Agitprop sets its apparatus into motion and carries out every campaign with a well-planned strategy. An example is this scheme, which was used to popularize the decisions of a party congress: The press and radio kicked off the campaign by publishing the official news release and colorful human-interest stories about the congress. In a day or two, the decisions were discussed in editorials, and roving reporters, visiting factories and kolkhozes all over the country, described the enthusiastic support of the workers. By then the proceedings of the congress were published in a booklet, put into the hands of the citizens, and discussed, first, at a meeting of activists, then at a "grand meeting" of the party, then at the regular party meetings, then at the meetings of trade unions, plants, and offices, and finally at the meetings of other mass organizations. Every citizen heard at least one propagandist explain the lessons of the recent congress. But this was still not enough.

Words alone do not satisfy the superego; actions are required. On this occasion, the subjects had to approve the decisions of the party, echo the ideas of the leaders and pass resolutions to that effect; they had to express their approval in letters, telegrams, and demonstrations. The miners' union, for instance, issued a manifesto urging the workers to join the current work competition—and so the miners did.[6] For two solid weeks the slogans saturated the population more thoroughly than the best advertising campaign can saturate the American people. And, if it suits the interest of the party state, the apparatus may keep a campaign alive for any length of time.

The propaganda machine always works in high gear and handles several nation-wide campaigns simultaneously. It creates a permanent frenzy of slogans and meetings, with good Communists running from one meeting to the next. The Day of the Railroad Workers, a ritual celebration actually lasting for two days, was solemnly marked with meetings, parades, athletic contests, exhibitions, and performances at the thousand largest railway stations of the country. On a hot summer Sunday in Hungary, when the temperature hovered near 100 degrees, the Agitprop still kept up the pace. The Workers' Guard had arranged three meetings of national importance and the Youth League only two, but that Sunday was the so-called Day of Co-operatives, and the efforts in this regard were more ambitious, drawing 50,000 people into a picnic park of the capital and producing meetings in three important cities and in every village of one province. The following Sunday turned out to be peaceful indeed, featuring not more than a few peace meetings (one in the capital and two in the provinces) and some "conferences" of the activists (five in the capital, three in the provinces). Constitution Day, which soon followed, was more tumultuous, with its 95 simultaneous grand meetings in the key cities of the state—which, in proportion to the population, are the equivalent of 1600 meetings in the United States.[7]

The central authority plans every propaganda activity and outlines all the details. This basic fact, however, must be ignored, and every citizen must behave as if he acted out of spontaneous enthusiasm, under the impulse of the slogan and his devotion to the party. Everybody has to contribute to the success of the campaign in his own way, showing his initiative, overfulfilling the official plan, and manifesting other public proofs of his loyalty. No zeal can be excessive. "Our agitation is sometimes too bashful," complained one functionary.[8] The good propagandist forgets about bashfulness and repeats the words of the Agitprop as if they were his own. The ambitious functionary tries to go beyond the instructions. A "sadistic party secretary" described by one informant demanded the loudest enthusiasm from those who were known to hate Communism the most. The fellow who had spent years in a labor camp had to carry a banner reading, "Long live the freedom of the proletariat."

Everybody seems to be trying to convince everybody else of the same idea. The official message is repeated from morning to night by innumerable voices. The variations are slight: the mass organizations express the message in popular terms, the Youth League adds a youthful touch, and the schoolteachers mouth a simplified version of it. It is still the same idea and the same style, a depressing sameness. Man's individual traits disappear behind this uniformity. The propagandists roar out their borrowed ideas in monotonous repetition. The masses, caught in a chain of propaganda, have to read the press, listen to the radio, attend the meetings, raise their hands, applaud, march, and work.

Western man evaluates human actions in terms of achievements and appraises persuasion by its efficiency. The advertising business in America tries to measure the objective success of a campaign in facts and figures and employs market research, copy testing, and sales analysis to get the most reliable answer. The Agitprop, however, has revealed no similar facts and figures on its own efficiency, because the logic of identification forbids objective measurement. The Agitprop people are not businessmen but devoted Communists, sincere believers in the Red philosophy. In their reasoning, identification is the final cause of the party: the party exists, consequently one has to be devoted to it. Loyalty precludes doubt and, therefore, it cannot be measured; any measurement would admit the possibility of doubt and would contradict the basic principle of identification. The Agitprop cannot imitate Madison Avenue, cannot move on the line of rational efficiency, cannot experiment with copy tests and questionnaires to find the most effective slogan and speech. Communist propaganda has to be ritualistic, cumbersome and awkward. Its efficiency should not be underestimated, nevertheless.

Observers in the West have repeatedly argued that the Red persuasion fails, since it does not transform every subject into a faithful Communist, but this is an argument that obviously oversimplifies the problem. Communist policy does not aim to convert all subjects. Such an aim would be impractical and undesirable and would be contrary to the hierarchic social order which presupposes more perfect and less perfect people. Communist propaganda has practical goals that correspond to the realities of life. It sets up two targets on two different levels. One target is the all-out conversion of a relatively small élite; the other is the partial inculcation of the masses with Soviet ideas.

When sizing up the efficiency of Red propaganda, one should not expect the incessant campaigns to end with the masses accurately perceiving and accepting all the slogans and messages. On the contrary, the average citizen is quite often hazy about the main objectives of the campaigns; the authorities rightly upbraid him as "ideologically backward," and he himself admits his ignorance with candor. This ignorance, however, does not mean that round-the-clock propaganda, carried out with an unabating intensity and with a totalitarian exclusion of all other messages, pours over him without leaving behind any effects.

The Soviet man is exposed to the same, ever-repeated ideas, he is helpless against the pressures of propaganda.

He may surrender to fatigue and apathy and drop the natural human resistance to persuasion. In those matters which are handled by official persuasion, he may give up his own reasoning, cease to develop his own ideas, renounce his critical judgment, and let the barrage of slogans block his own thinking. As one informant put it, "Man gets muffled by the propaganda, becomes drugged and stupefied as if he were drunk." This is not the intoxication of elation; it is rather the fatalism induced by every Oriental tyranny. In this state, the ego lowers its conscious controls, accepts the necessity, and absorbs the thoughts forced upon it. Communist propaganda campaigns inevitably deposit some ideas in the minds of the populace, in much the same way as flowing water deposits its silt. This ideological silt that is left behind is the main achievement of Communist propaganda.

To be sure, the citizen absorbs only some insignificant fragments, a few words of a slogan or some modest particles of an argument. But he cannot put out of his mind what is repeated obstinately, and after many campaigns the accumulated rudiments in his mind will constitute an unorganized body of principles. They will not amount to a perfect knowledge of the official philosophy or to a complete identification with the Red superego; but they will amount to a partial knowledge and identification. The ordinary citizen will be influenced to a certain extent, persuaded of some principles, made a believer of some slogans. In other areas he may remain a disbeliever, a grumbling, doubting, dissatisfied critic, but his individual superego will never be the same as it was before the impact of the propaganda. He will be influenced to a degree, and he will make a compromise between his own individual beliefs and the basic Communist ideas. He will show that amount of belief which is expected from the imperfect but amenable masses who are under the guidance of the cadre people.

All-out conversion is always limited to small numbers, to those few people who are searching for convictions. Such people are susceptible to persuasion and may discover in the teachings of the party the ultimate goal of their search. Communism skillfully inclines its propaganda towards them, finds enough converts in their ranks to recruit the necessary number of dedicated followers, and fills its cadre with real fanatics. As more campaigns roll over the population, as new Communist-educated generations are produced, the penetration of the masses becomes more complete and the conversion of the susceptible individuals more frequent. The Red leaders know how to influence people, and whenever their persuasion falls short of the desired results, they resort to force and let command do what propaganda is unable to.

VIII. THE TERROR OF THE PERFECT ONES

One of the stories I collected is identified by the sentimental title, "Forgive Me." It is short, ironic, and grim. Its hero had been languishing in jail for years when one day the door of his cell opened just for a moment to admit a new cell mate. The new prisoner had made only a few hesitating steps into the dim cell when the old-timer recognized him as a former friend who had later alienated the affections of his wife and destroyed his marital bliss. The newcomer, conscious of his guilt, stopped with a jerk and whispered haltingly, "Can you forgive me for what I have done to you?" Whereupon the old inmate sat up on his bunk and answered with a grin, "You should forgive me for what I shall do to you. I am the cadre secretary of the prisoners, and I shall report you to the warden."

This story implies that there is no forgiveness and there are no innocent people in Communist society. Everybody sins, but under constraint. The concepts of guilt and innocence are washed away. All suffer nightmares of guilt and ask for forgiveness; but, deprived of their liberty, they are unable to mend their ways. A sense of guilt and the inability to atone haunt the Soviet conscience and constitute the psychological basis of the Red system of terror.

I

Command has many forms, each of them differing from the others in degree of rigor. Sometimes command works with the ferocity of the Queen of Hearts, whose readiness to chop off heads has been shared by many tyrants of history. At other times it makes people conform merely by threat of force; this method of procuring obedience was the Utopian ideal of many philosophers and perhaps actually existed in the idyllic life of some Pacific Islands. In the field of government, these two extremes are well exemplified by the contrast of democracy and autocracy.

Democracies seriously endeavor to restrict the use of command. In America, for example, command has disappeared (at least to a remarkable extent) from the social contacts of private life. The executive and his underlings do their best to "co-operate" rather than to "command and obey," and the executive, in fact, often goes out of his way to avoid the appearance of commanding. The political philosophy of democracy generally divides life into two domains: the public domain in which compliance with law is required and the private domain into which law must not encroach. In public life, law has the full vigor of command, provided it stays within its prescribed limitations. Although the recent idea of the welfare state has vastly extended the public domain and restricted the private one, a democratic society recoils from expanding its law-making power over the citizens' sentiments and beliefs. Autocratic societies, on the other hand, reject the fine distinction between private and public domains. They systematically resort to command, use power in all areas of life, and demand identification with a ruler, dictator, political doctrine, or belief. The autocracy of old times represented not only a form of government but also a compulsory superego. Czarism tried to impose a creed centering around the Czar as the father of his people and its efforts in this direction were so cruel that it was labeled "the petrification of the Terror."[1]

The nineteenth century saw the progress of democracy and the decay of autocracy. It succumbed to a magnificent illusion. It hoped that in the course of a peaceful development enlightened democracy would finally triumph all over the world. Unfortunately, our own century brought a quick end to this golden dream. The Armageddon did not end in the victory of democracy. The place of the stiff, old autocrats was occupied by new and nimble dictators who, although less secure in the possession of power, followed their masters in the ruthless application of command. Our era has seen the rise, and also the fall, of a great many dictators who, with a frightening alacrity, have filled out every vacuum in political power. It should be particularly noted that dictatorships existed in those countries which are now the satellites of Moscow. Communism has not been established on the ruins of democracy but on the debris of slowly collapsing autocracies and fickle dictatorships.

The rise of modern dictatorship was greatly aided by some characteristic social forces of our century. The inventions of technology, the improvement of the communication systems, the scientific co-ordination of human work, increased the efficiency of command. They stripped the individual of his former independence and delivered him unarmed to that agency which organized command, the state. Communism, for its part, did not fail to recognize the significance of the new forces. It put the whole technology in the service of command and quoted with approval Marx's dictum about force being the midwife of every new society.[2] From its beginning, the Bolshevik state has practiced a bloody midwifery. It has no illusions but uses command in the same totalitarian fashion as it uses propaganda. It mobilizes all means that can effectively facilitate the flow of command from the top to the bottom; it reaches all subjects and harshly breaks down any resistance to its will.

Modern technology and human engineering helped the totalitarian state to establish a more complete control of conscience than has ever existed before. They helped the new Leviathan to watch and judge all subjects, to keep an eye upon the private and civic lives of the citizens, record all their actions worthy of attention, make people accountable for their past, and punish all those who lack the required degree of loyalty.

During this process the police became established as a new institution of the state. It happened in the Era of Enlightenment that such monarchs of good will as Frederick II of Prussia and Maria Theresa of Austria began to police their subjects in the hope of promoting a general betterment.[3] They entrusted the duty of watching the citizens to new police institutions that performed the job impersonally and scientifically. Soon the notorious police ministers Fouché and Sedlnitzky developed large bureaucracies to spy upon everybody. Czarism regarded the police as an essential part of Holy Russia. The Third Division of the Czar's chancery watched people in their private and public lives, employed *agents provocateurs,* fomented discontent and suppressed it, and played cat-and-mouse games with the subjects. Police agent Azev organized his own revolutionary group and eventually assassinated the minister of the Czar. In the present satellite countries, notably in Hungary and Rumania, the pre-Communist dictatorships kept the private lives of citizens under surveillance and jailed people for a political joke or for a love affair disapproved of by the government.

Communism inherited this organization and improved it, making the supervision of subjects more effective. Under the Czars any service rendered to the police was a service to Holy Russia. Now, under Communism, it is everybody's legal duty to help the police, to report the errors of fellow citizens and to seek their punishment by the authorities. The criminal code of the Russian Soviet Republic imposes imprisonment up to ten years for failure to report "treason" or any "counterrevolutionary crime."[4] As a matter of fact, reporting is more than a legal duty, it is a moral obligation.

Every wrongdoer is an enemy of the people, one of those many demons who fill the world. And "vigilance" in the face of ever-present evil is a cardinal virtue of Communist morality. Everybody has to watch everybody else. "Be vigilant," warns the poet, "every man is suspect!" The citizen, however, cannot take up a single-handed fight against the devils; only the authorities are strong enough to defeat these mighty demons. It is, therefore, everybody's duty to report anything that might be worth the attention of the authorities: every negligence, fault, mistake, and breach of faith. No detail, however small, should be overlooked. The Hungarian minister of justice himself called upon the citizens to denounce more speculators.[5]

Indeed, the citizens do watch and report, under pressure or voluntarily, out of a sense of duty or as a result of competition, hatred, or aggression. The reports, signed or unsigned, written or verbal, may be handed to any functionary or member of the party, forwarded directly to the organs of the state administration, or deposited in the suggestion boxes at the places of work. But denunciation is a work too serious to be left in the hands of amateurs and dilettantes. Professionals do a more skillful, systematic job, and the Communist state employs all kinds of professionals. Many activists work as "house trustees," "block trustees," or "people's controllers" and in such capacities keep an eye upon neighbors and strangers, private citizens and officials alike.

Many of these spies are at work, and their reports, in due course, reach one of the two main controlling agencies of the party state: the cadre department or the police. One or the other of these agencies has a personal file on every citizen, containing his employment record, his "political profile," and information about his class origin, church attendance, and family life. Facts and gossip are recorded with equal zeal, and the incoming reports are very superficially evaluated. As a result, the personal files contain much false information, and those few police reports that have been published impress the reader as unreliable, vague, and clumsy.[6]

Oriental secrecy surrounds the records. No citizen knows what his file contains or how suspect he may be to the authorities. The watching of people is a one-sided affair. Everybody is under suspicion, and the evidence against everybody is always being collected, but nobody can answer the charges or submit his defense. Everybody can expect some incriminating entries on his record, but nobody can guess how and when the information will be used to his detriment. The personal file is a menace threatening everybody, creating insecurity and fear.

After all, man does not express all his ideas and feelings but keeps some of them to himself. Everybody has secrets or half-secrets which he reveals only to a few intimates. An introvert may have more and better-guarded secrets, while an extrovert may give his away easily, but everybody has secrets. Communism, however, denies the individual's right to keep secrets. The party alone has the right to be secretive, and not its subjects. The citizen should reveal himself to the authorities, and silence is a sign of insufficient loyalty.

Nobody can escape the watching eyes of the party. Nobody can hope that his guilt will go undetected. Those who are imperfect and guilty may be given away by any display of their inner selves. They can trust only the negative defenses: silence, cunning, duplicity. "Hold your place," a poet counseled his readers, "and do your job without words." A Communist newspaper reporter was flabbergasted to find that workers, who obviously had some complaints, did not speak up but kept repeating the proverb, "Speech is silver but silence is golden."[7] Talk, to be sure, is a usual reaction to stress, and any tension is greatly relieved by "talking it out." The vassal of Communism, however, must suppress his natural reactions and must relegate many experiences into the nonconscious. He has to narrow down his consciousness and keep it within the limits mapped by the superego. As one informant put it, "One has to vegetate, to live like a plant."

If consciousness is reduced by artificial means, man cannot help talking a language of inhibitions. He repeats the safe commonplaces, and becomes inhibited when he reaches a topic about which he feels sincere emotion and personal involvement. The Communist subject is often unable to express clearly his personal grievances but repeats certain clichés which do not necessarily apply to his case. His inhibited talk cannot be easily translated into "free speech." Thus, the Western man frequently misunderstands the talk of Communist subjects as revealing underdeveloped, primitive, poorly educated minds. He is prone to think of the people under Communist rule in popular stereotypes that emphasize mental backwardness or perhaps the image of the noble savage.

As the subject cannot talk, his tensions and frustrations mount and, in the usual ways, are transformed into aggression. The aggressive energies accumulated in the masses have to be drained off. The Bolshevik system opens up one flood gate only and channels these energies in one direction —against the fellow citizens. All other exits are locked, but the denunciation of fellow citizens is a meritorious way of releasing aggression. Thus, the general institution of policing and spying gains strength from itself and creates that psychological state which is necessary for its continuing existence.

This officially approved form of aggression should not deceive us as to the basically depressive character of the Soviet citizen's experience. The subject who is constantly watched, who is not free to talk or be silent, feels humiliation and inferiority. He is impotent. One informant spoke of feeling the way the snail must when he is climbing a huge tree for the green leaves of the crown. The tiny subject is measured by the standards of the merciless superego, fashioned for supermen rather than for imperfect humans. He cannot fulfill the standards, cannot escape errors and sins. His past is never forgotten but is recorded in his file; and his sins are never forgiven, but he may be prosecuted for them at any time. An impending danger hovers over everybody, and there is no refuge from it because Soviet laws are not protective guardians but frightening ghosts, alarming apparitions.

II

One piece of legislation in the law books may be the best rule that can be applied under a given set of circumstances, another piece may be silly or incomprehensible; but the whole body of the law is always the extension of a legal philosophy, one part of a superego. Legal systems and constitutions show some of the same characteristics as the superegos.

In the Western democracies, law represents the opinion of the majority expressed in a constitutional way. The constitution assures the citizen's equal right to make law and tacitly assumes that this law will be an ideal compromise between what is morally right and what is in the best interest of the individuals. Laws must be promulgated for the information of all, and no secrecy is tolerated in legal administration or the judiciary. Actions which constitute a crime are clearly defined. Guilt or innocence is adjudged by independent courts; the prosecution has to submit concrete evidence, and the accused must have his legal defense. Altogether, this legal system is clear, logical, and stable and grants the citizen the maximum security within his rights.

In the Soviet system, the party state is not only the administrator of the law but also its maker and its supreme judge. Laws and statutes are created by the party under the assumption that the interest of the party is the interest of the subjects and that lawmaking should consider nothing but the convenience of the party. "There is, and there can be, no real constitutional limitation on governmental power, since the constitution in its interpretation and application is subject to governmental power." Thus, constitutions are "looked upon as ephemeral phenomena which—so the Communists claim—reflect the prevailing conditions and which are designed to be replaced by new documents at the next major step of the country's journey toward a socialistic-communistic society."[8]

Within such an unstable framework, the legal norms are changeable and hazy. Laws duly passed by the parliament are rather few in number and are often insignificant in content. The Communist parliament is a ritual body, meeting infrequently and passing laws which are lofty manifestoes removed from practical life. The legal norms that regulate daily life are defined in a multitude of extra-parliamentary statutes, in "decrees with the force of law," "resolutions," "decrees," and "directives" issued by the Presidium of the parliament, the Council of Ministers, and the various ministries. The governmental organs have an absolute right to make law at their will, without consulting the representatives of the citizens. The decrees and directives are published at large only when the issuing authority wishes to do so; many of them are labeled "confidential" and withheld from the public. The citizen is bound by a great number of secret statutes and is supposed to observe legal norms unknown and inaccessible to him.

Cicero's old saying, "more laws—less justice," has never

been more applicable. Soviet jurisprudence, which grew out of the arbitrariness of Czarist despotism, defines the most important concepts hazily and demolishes the safe borderlines between crime and legality. Its basic principle is loyal identification with the regime. As the Stalinist constitution of the U.S.S.R. euphemistically phrases it, the citizen has "honestly to perform public duties, and to respect the rules of socialist intercourse" (Article 130). Identification, however, originates in nonconscious needs and desires; therefore, it cannot be clearly defined and subjected to jurisprudence. In the lack of precision, almost any action may be interpreted as a sign of insufficient loyalty and even as a "political crime," because in a totalitarian state almost any action has a political significance. Guilt and innocence are vague concepts; the definition of crime is improvised and changes with the turns of the policy. A fictional Bolshevik, heroic leader of a local Cheka, justifies himself with a pithy statement: "I was right in shooting a hundred prisoners without taking into consideration their guilt or innocence, because guilt or innocence in your Philistine sense of the word does not exist for me."[9]

In actual practice, the authorities define crime by examining each case separately. As a rule of thumb, however, crime is everything that amounts to deviation from the official philosophy and opposition to the existing order of power. Thus, negligence in production, absenteeism, failure to fulfill the plan, and similar deficiencies in labor discipline are subject to criminal prosecution, and anybody who appears to be successful in making money is investigated as a possible speculator. A political joke may conceivably be the crime of "rumor spreading," i.e., the dissemination of news not contained in the official news releases. Mere association may also be suspicious: the guilt of his loved ones, relatives, and protegés may cast doubt on any person, and, when crime is committed, the whole "criminal chain" of relatives and friends has to be punished.[10]

Since almost any act may be a crime, nobody knows the extent of his guilt. Fiction has often played with the problem of a conscience lost in ignorance. Franz Kafka created a nightmarish world in which crime is "assigned," in which laws and courts are elusive phantoms, and in which the conscience cannot decide its guilt and innocence. But long before Freud, Joyce, and Kafka, Russian literature liked to depict the bad conscience which could not remember its guilt. A heroine of Gogol spoke about a terrifying dream from which something was evidently missing. Whereupon a friend answered, "No wonder that you did not dream of a great many things. You do not even know a tenth part of what your soul knows." Dostoevsky's hero, an innocent and harmless daydreamer, complained with no reason whatsoever of the "gloomy, sullen gnawing of conscience," and Tolstoy on a well-known occasion dreamed that he was both the executioner and executed. The perceptions of these littérateurs could not have been entirely alien to life. A torturing conscience which did not know its guilt, which submissively accepted the guilty verdict without querying the justification of the verdict, might have been common under Czarist terror and Orthodox mysticism. The idea of "we have not yet suffered enough" has been repeatedly put on the lips of the muzhik, and the pressure of the unknown guilt was the central experience of the humble religious sect of the Doukhobors just as of some intellectual revolutionary circles.[11]

Communism took this collective feeling of guilt and fitted it into its own system. Guilt comes from imperfection in realizing the superego, and nobody but the leaders can be perfect. Hence, it behooves the Soviet man to acknowledge his guilt, and official praise is given to the former "counter-revolutionary" who speaks up and says in a loud voice, "I want to be punished."[12] In this form, the motif of the unknown guilt assumes a practical role and figures in a crucial phase of the terror system, the investigation of crimes.

An art critic, writing on the architecture of a newly erected police headquarters building, remarked, "It is true that the Communist police are friendly and cheerful, but at the same time they express forcefully the real significance [of the Soviet system], discipline."[13] Indeed, the police are an integral part of the state administration, they are the strong-armed guardians of the superego. They are not only the keepers of law and order but also the uncompromising representatives of the party state in all the activities of the citizens. Police, as the general agents of the strict disciplinary system, exert the main social control in every nook and corner of the Red empire, watch the people, apply the current interpretation of law, and pick, accordingly, the necessary number of criminals out of the population.

Whatever the police do is the rightful law. Civic agencies, public opinion, and the press have no power to supervise and restrict their work. The suspect, in particular, has no rights against the police. As one Minister of Justice stated: "Our fatherland does not accord freedom to the enemies of the People's Republic."[14] The arrested person may spend months and years in jail, cut off from the outer world and from any aid that would contribute to his legal defense and his physical and psychological well-being. He may disappear without a trace behind the thick walls of the police headquarters, utterly at the mercy of his guards. He may be subjected to any degree of deprivation and torture. If he can resist physical torture, he may be broken by psychological torments, for example, by the knowledge that the police have power over him for an unlimited time, even beyond possible sentence or acquittal.

He is defenseless against such powers. The police are

free to manipulate him methodically and effectively, to turn him into an obedient servant of the disciplinary system. They may apply against him the instruments of terror, using them with a sophisticated psychology, with certain techniques designed to subdue the human material. Their most notorious technique annihilates the victim's own superego and substitutes for it the norms and values of the police. This "brainwashing" is by no means a Communist invention. It was used by the Czarist police and by the many dictators of Eastern Europe, but the Bolshevik system perfected it.[15]

Communist police refined their techniques of brainwashing through practice and came upon a principle that is used in legitimate psychiatric treatments. A great and sudden shock affects a man's whole personality and may change its structure for any length of time. In brainwashing the police change the victim's personality according to plan by administering repeated shocks: physical torture and psychological stress and strain. The superhuman requirements of the superego, the merciless enforcement of these requirements, the uneasiness of the bad conscience which does not remember its guilt, the complete isolation and secrecy which surround the victim, all contribute to the final aim. As additional and unexpected shocks, the victim is confronted with the secrets that have been collected in his personal files, with threats against his family and friends, with sudden promises of leniency and clemency, and with a treatment capriciously alternating between severe brutality and apparent sympathy. At one point of this psychological manipulation, fear takes hold of him, a fear that soon may outgrow the limits of tolerance.

Nobody is immune to fear, since it is a manifold experience. The natural desire to avoid pain is just one simple form of it, and many people are unafraid of physical pain. Another form of fear appears whenever the ego expects the loss of something highly valued by it. Since everybody cherishes values, everybody has areas of fear. Whoever is fearless of torture may be fearful of an injury to his family; whoever scorns death may be much affected by the possibility of losing his faith in a superego. In brainwashing the police carefully find out what the victim's specific area of fear is and work upon it. Stalwart party members, unafraid of torture but sensitive on the point of their Communist honor, are broken by confronting them with the errors they committed in their past service of the party; and a cardinal of the Catholic Church was dragged into a room and compelled to watch "the most obscene orgies." [16]

The police, by constantly reminding the victim of his defenseless state, by filling him with a maximum insecurity, bring him to a point at which his extreme fear releases a psychological chain reaction. They annihilate his feeling of personal security, reduce his self-respect, throw out of balance his self-concept and his "character." The victim is tossed around like a plaything and cannot regard himself any longer as a free agent leading a self-chosen way of life. His notion (common to all men) that he is the center of his own world must be renounced. He loses his human identity and is ready to deny his inner self. At the end of the process, his personality is disintegrated and his individual superego annihilated.

The disintegration of the personality does not necessarily affect consciousness, and the victim may be well aware of the changes. He can observe, some times lucidly, how his inner self is broken down. "It was," as one victim recalled this process, "as if I had been put into a madhouse and had to act like the inmates around me. After a while I was not sure whether I was normal and the world around me insane, or the world was normal and I had lost my senses. I was obsessed by the idea that I had left my body and it had been taken up by my grandmother who had died insane. At one point of madness, I had to make sure that I was still a male. . . . It was the most excruciating experience. I wept afterwards like a child." It is always painful when an outside force changes one's personality. Even patients under regular psychotherapeutic treatment (administered with care and caution) complain of the pain. In the brutality of police treatment, the many dreadful elements add up to an intolerable experience.

Through this painful procedure the victim's personality is changed, his superego demolished or injured, and a psychological vacuum created. Now the second phase of the brainwashing may start. Although it is less painful, it is the phase in which the desired end of the manipulation is achieved. In this phase it is possible to inject new norms and values or to build up an entirely new superego in the victim. He has nothing to rely on and is susceptible to any suggestion offered to him. His resistance is broken, his autonomous existence is lost, and he is unwilling, or unable, to guide his own actions. He will talk and behave in accordance with the superego imposed upon him; he will, in brief, comply with the wishes of the police.

In order to escape further torture, many victims yield to the manipulation with a minimum of resistance. They do not try to defend their inner selves but surrender and comply with any demand made upon them. They turn into facile instruments of the police, informers, false witnesses, and, sometimes, seemingly enthusiastic stooges of Communism. They feign and dissemble, outwardly consenting to any demand, however contrary it may be to their own principles. The greater the victim's personal involvement in his own superego, the more resistance he puts up against brainwashing. Those who are unwilling to feign, who are dedicated to an idea, who do not compromise, have to suffer most.

Few people have an ego strong enough to resist this manipulation. When it is over, most victims are ready to sign any confession prepared by the police and to "recite it like a memorized lesson" before any court. The police regularly utilize this willingness and fabricate confessions, nay, entire crimes. The "construction trial" is rather common in Bolshevik justice. Whenever it is politically expedient, the police "construct" a crime: a plot to overthrow the regime, sabotage, espionage, any wildly fantastic scheme such as the Moscow doctors' conspiracy to murder their patients. Then, those people who can, or must, be involved in the scheme, to whom a crime is assigned, are arrested and the police work on them to "accept the construction." The police are usually successful. The accused, whether guilty or not, stand always alone, unaided by law or by their fellow beings, lonely figures against the total might of the political system.[17]

Communist philosophy approves of assigned crimes and construction trials, since it denies the free will of humans. "The doctrine of freedom of the will," said Bukharin, "is a semi-religious view which contradicts all the facts of life."[18] Personal autonomy is also discarded. Nothing but his utility to the party justifies the existence of the individual. His aims, values, and goals must be blotted out, he must follow orders blindly and serve the interest of the party state. If the party requires it, he must lie and accuse himself of crimes never committed. If he is more useful as a prisoner, he must confess and go to jail. If he is more useful dead than alive, he must die. As an immutable principle, he must accept his assigned role.

Before this principle, the Communist hierarchy itself breaks down and yields to equality. Leaders from the upper cadre, rank-and-file nonentities, and lowly outsiders have equally been accused of a constructed crime. In the treatment given to them, no difference existed, although their final attitude may have differed. The opponent of Communism may have gone to his death with the knowledge that he had foreseen the essential brutality of the system, whereas many devoted party members may have marched proudly to the gallows to seal there irrevocably their identification with the party.

III

The absolute power of the police is limited only by the inherent imperfections of the system. Since crime is the lack of identification, the number of criminals is so large that all of them cannot be apprehended. As a further snag, the police cannot decide any better than the cadre department who is "perfect" and who is not. Thus, they follow a practical course, selecting out of the many poorly identified subjects a certain number of victims and prosecuting them. Those unlucky ones who have to suffer the terror are picked at random or because of a revengeful denunciation or political expediency.

As the official policy makes its tactical turns, the periods of intense terror alternate with periods of relaxation. In Hungary, for example, a three-year period of terror (1950-53) was followed by the liberal "New Course" that relaxed the police surveillance and released many arrested people; then, in 1955-56, the terror was renewed, and the police smashed fifteen major and thirty minor counter-revolutionary organizations.[19] The cycles of police terror do not necessarily coincide with the cycles of party purges and membership drives; but some political cycle is waxing or waning all the time, whipping up fear and insecurity and stamping life under Communism with the characteristic marks of instability.

The work of the police adapts itself to these general policies, and the number of arrests is determined not by the crimes actually committed but by the momentary requirements of the cycle. In the terror phase, faithful Communists may be apprehended but a small-scale opposition activity may go undetected. One informant, who had been engaged in "illegal" work directed against the party, was arrested and found to his great surprise that his anti-Communist activities remained unknown to the police. He was charged with misapplication of merchandise in his job as a warehouse supervisor. In this tragicomic case, the police investigation discovered that the charge originated in a bookkeeping error and no material was missing—our informant was released after three weeks in prison. The police system is by no means foolproof but tries to cover its shortcomings with cruelty rather than with leniency. The mistreatment of criminals is a case in point.

Communist penology views the criminal as a demonic enemy who must be exorcised and forced to surrender before the representatives of the superego. It has, accordingly, two practical goals: procuring reparation for the crime and re-educating the criminal.[20] The twofold task, not humanitarian in itself, is entrusted to the ubiquitous police. In their hands, obtaining reparation for crimes becomes a cruel fight against the demons, a fight that employs the weapons of pain and humiliation. Through his suffering, the criminal repays what he owes to society and the evil spirit is expelled from his body. The demon is exorcised, and the prisoner can then be re-educated into a loyal citizen. Hard work carried out under harsh commands is the best re-education, and the Communist penal system is, in general, connected with forced labor.

Punitive labor has its historical origins. In nineteenth-century Russia, one popular school of moral philosophy glorified the spiritual purification and ethical improvement that come from frugality, hard physical labor, and austere living. Dostoevsky, Tolstoy, and a score of other moralists decried the amenities of urban civilization as the cradle of sin and extolled the crude but idyllic life of the peasants as the fruitful source of golden virtues. The Czarist government and the pre-Communist dictatorships in Eastern Europe were hardly concerned with the moral improvement of their subjects but wanted to perpetuate their regimes. They distorted this moral philosophy and cynically established penal colonies and labor camps.

Communism, with its passion for organization, perfected the scheme. Such official organs as the GULAG in the Soviet Union and the KÖMI in Hungary employed huge armies of forced laborers who worked in the most unattractive jobs of mining, construction, and lumbering. Their work, as Western economists argue, was economically unprofitable, wasting labor, skills, and capital investment. The size of the forced labor pool changed not in accordance with the economic demand but with the cycles of terror and relaxation.[21] Evidently, Communism pursues other than economic goals. It is guided by the principle that the inmate of the labor camp is fulfilling the requirements of the Red morality of work, so that, eventually, he may qualify as a free citizen again.

This principle leads to further absurdities. Any waste in forced labor is regarded not as an economic loss but as a ritualistic sacrifice to the superego. The authorities silently tolerate the dreadful toll that overwork and exposure take among the prisoners because suffering and death are just accessories of the re-education process. The prisoner can prove his innocence by being content in his place and working as hard as the authorities require. Discontent can only prove that he deserves further punishment and should not be released. And indeed, he may be held beyond the expiration of his formal sentence, held until that indefinite time when he is judged to be re-educated.

IV

As the old dictum has it, the more laws that exist, the smaller the respect they command, and the stronger the police force, the more frequently the law is broken. The case of the Soviet World corrobrates this. The Communist Leviathan ended the exploitation of workers by capitalists and by the very same act expected to eradicate crime, too. Life, however, refuted this doctrinaire reasoning, and crime did not vanish with the expropriation of the means of production. Numerous decrees and directives are circumvented or broken, and the number of crimes committed is great—in spite of the stern discipline. Evidently, the subjects do not live up to the high requirements of the superego.

This is the case with "social property," that is, the property of state-owned enterprises. According to all available information, the same people who have due respect for "private property" regularly pilfer "social property." One poet exclaimed with disgust, "The citizens steal, cheat, and burglarize." Newspapers report shocking thefts and embezzlements. In one factory, within six months 1,115 thieves were uncovered, although in the opinion of the party secretary not more than five out of every hundred thieves were seized. One worker was seized when walking out of the plant with two front doors. A doctor reported that patients left the hospital taking entire beds with them. "Communists and functionaries," lamented the press, "knew about these things and even took part in the transactions."[22] All sources agree that stealing is more prevalent in the state-owned Communist economy that it was in the formerly private enterprises.

The authorities fight theft with all possible means. The official measures, however, are of no avail. The usual techniques of the party fail conspicuously because mass stealing has a powerful, deeply embedded motivation. The inhibition against stealing is natural to the respectable citizenry; but if everybody is regarded as a potential criminal, why should anyone refrain from stealing? Workers getting an adequate wage do not steal as a means of obtaining their livelihood. But in Communist countries consumer goods are scarce and such necessities as nails, lumber, housewares, or plumbing supplies cannot regularly be obtained in stores. Needy people may take unlawful possession of many things they need. The hierarchical structure of Communist society removes further inhibitions, and the little fellow in the plant argues that "people above us steal even more."[23] And finally, people very often steal as premeditated sabotage, as a silent demonstration against the system. Many subjects placate their consciences by committing acts which they know are crimes.

The case of prostitution is similar. According to Communist theory, prostitution is a sin of capitalism and the prostitute a victim of bourgeois exploitation; therefore, vice cannot exist in Soviet society. The party, to be sure, is actually prudish in matters of sex, much the same way as Victorian England was. Several times it has closed down the brothels and announced the successful liquidation of venal love. Prostitution, however, seems to be more than a form of capitalistic exploitation or a social illness that can be remedied by prudish morals. It defies official measures and flourishes in all cities. The police regularly raid those places of amusement which are frequented by soliciting girls and punish their crimes with internment. Still, they are unable to eradicate vice. The arrested girls are replaced by new ones, and the disorderly houses are secretly reopened, time and time again. In the city of Budapest, within one or two months the police closed down thirty to forty places of prostitution, and one night's raid netted "several dozen streetwalkers."[24]

A disciplinary system cannot create the state of innocence. The Soviet citizen spends his life among many criminals and even more potential criminals. He lives in a world in which guilt and innocence have no limits and in which terror is a natural part of state administration. If he gets caught in the chain of terror agencies, he is carried away and manipulated in the same mechanical way as a piece of raw material is handled on the assembly line. The assembly line of terror picks up and carries off all kinds of people, opponents of the regime, neutrals, and a great many true Communists also.

The sight of innocent victims, however, cannot alarm the faithful Communist. An American admirer of the U.S.S.R. commented, "People who are conscious of innocence and fight for it will eventually come back." The hero of a novel, jailed unjustly for years, did not feel insulted, not even angry, but compared his sufferings to the punishment that a child receives from his loving mother. "Why!" he reflected, "did you nurture anger against your mother who scorned and smacked you wrongfully just because some neighbors and relatives had calumniated you? Is it possible to be angry at a mother? . . . If the Communist is hit on his head by a flagpole, he still remains faithful to the flag." An unjust persecution is just one of those trials which is supposed to turn the good Communist into a better one. The devoted party man does not even defend himself against the charges of the party, since they, even though unfounded, can only further his perfection.[25]

Since the party is the source of morality, any contact with it, be it painful or pleasant, must be edifying. If one may believe Communist literature, the party has done miracles in morally elevating its subjects. The mere contact with the Plant Disciplinary Committee cures (according to one story) the alcoholic. In an allegedly true story, a young worker, addicted to an old widow and the cups and on his way to skid row, was reformed under the influence of the Young Communist League. Nothing is more elevating than the state plan, and one hero of Soviet fiction "has fallen in love with his job during the first Five-Year Plan."[26] In the Communist view, there is no terror, just a disciplinary system. This social discipline, so the Communists argue, is exercised by the perfect ones for the benefit of the party state; it is necessary and useful to curb the wicked, to keep people on the right path and help them to proceed on the road to perfection. It is a regular means of making Soviet men.

The Western mind rejects this reasoning as a cruel and barbarous theorem, born of the depravity or sadism of the Red leaders. Yet, the Western mind is somewhat at a loss to understand the seeming complacency with which the subjects of the Soviet empire tolerate the terror. To be sure, suffering works with a strange psychology. What does suffering mean to people? No two men could agree on an answer. He who feels his guilt wishes to suffer for it and is often willing to take more torment than would be the reasonable atonement for his sin. For him, suffering is not suffering but reparation and terror is not terror but discipline: the stricter the better. In order to atone he is willing to face deprivations, renounce the amenities of life, and take a lowly position at the feet of the privileged classes. He shows all the symptoms of the pariah psychology that leads so many people of the East to accept their plight without bitterness or protest.

V

At this point it is necessary to note a new turn in the Soviet policy. The system of terror described in the previous pages characterized the Communist empire up to the middle of the 1950's; then a policy of liberalization set in that is usually associated with the name of Khrushchev. It remains to be seen whether this policy represents only a transitory period of relaxation similar to those which had occurred in the time of Stalin also and had been followed by another wave of terror, or whether it signals a new course in the operation of Communism in which the use of terror is restricted and fear is not so much applied as the milder forms of psychological manipulation. Whatever the answer, the new policy greatly relaxed the old system of watching the citizens, permitted certain new forms of criticism, emphasized the due process of law in its Soviet sense, restricted the power of the police authorities, reduced the number of political crimes, and attempted to eliminate such instruments of terror as forced labor and the construction trial.

Many of these changes were carried out informally, since the Soviet system knows all too well how to operate through untraceable directives which leak from the top offices of leadership down to the local authorities of the villages. Other changes were officially proclaimed and even highly publicized. A series of decrees reclassified as misdemeanors many acts that formerly had been defined as crimes, another directive ordered that cadre files be maintained only on persons in leadership positions and not on ordinary citizens. In the same fashion, it was widely publicized that a newly established surveillance office was set up with a civic-minded rather than punitive aim and that the "voluntary policemen" of the department of motor vehicles were appointed not for the prosecution but for the assistance of the intoxicated driver, for putting him in the back seat and driving him safely home.[27]

The Soviet man could read many encouraging announcements in the press, yet one may question how much his sense of security increased over the years. The policy of liberalization did not follow a straight path, but progressed on one line and reverted again to harsher measures on another line. The new liberal policy had hardly been initiated when, in the summer of 1957, Soviet Russia and some of the satellite countries declared war on the "parasites" and, in order to secure a much-needed increase in the size of the labor force, resorted to extra-legal means against idlers, speculators, and other people without steady employment. They authorized village and street meetings of the citizens (acting under the benevolent guidance of the local party organization) to sentence summarily all who avoided "socially useful work" and lived on "unearned income."

In other cases, the local authorities seemed to be reluctant in committing themselves to the liberal course. High officials repeatedly pledged the rehabilitation of those who had been previously indicted, and, as a matter of fact, much was done in this respect. Yet, officials decided to exclude from high school a fourteen-year-old village boy because his parents were of "unstable political attitude" and he himself was involved in a reproachable childish prank. As another case in point, the surveillance of the population was greatly relaxed, yet some of the authorities still insist that they must know every detail of the citizens' private lives. When a white-collar worker applied for a better apartment, the proper authorities turned him down on grounds of misrepresentation: at the official hearing he failed to mention that he had some savings and planned to buy a car.[28]

These and many similar inconsistencies indicate that the cruelty of the Stalin era is gone, but the Soviet man is still supposed to live under a disciplinary system. The Khrushchev regime may very well feel that its hold over the citizens is strong enough to make extreme terror unnecessary; but at the same time it firmly believes that the party state must be the great taskmaster, prodding and guiding the mass of imperfect citizens. The new policy is far from aiming at freedom in the Western sense of the word; yet, it has made a tremendous impact upon the masses, particularly in the satellite countries. One may speculate on the extent of this impact, and the speculation should begin by realizing the essence of the recent changes: the first generation of Soviet man was forged by Lenin and Stalin through an ample use of terror; but now, unless the general policy makes another turn, the second generation will be produced with much less suffering, through a relatively pleasant manipulation.

The peoples of Russia, who furnished the first generation, were used to all forms of terror, unleashed by the Czars and Communist leaders alike. They came from a culture in which public self-humiliation was a natural part of man's plight, in which the feeling of unknown guilt was very much alive and stern punishment by one's superiors was meekly accepted. Many of them regarded suffering as reparation and terror as discipline, accepted whatever came their way without much bitterness, and viewed the Soviet police state as the agency of atonement.

Those peoples in the satellite countries who were to be molded into the second generation came from a very different background. They, too, had lived under native dictatorships and often in police states which had not been any better than Communism; but oppression in itself does not necessarily change the psychological characteristics of people. In their case, the native culture (or for that matter, the national character) strikingly differed from the Russian patterns. The Czechs, Hungarians, Poles, different as they are in language and mores, resemble one another in their strong repugnance to public humiliation, in their relative freedom from guilt feelings, and in their stubborn resistance to the punishing hand of the powerful. Their national culture demands a strong assertion of the ego before the public, emphasizes an autonomy in the actions of the individual, and, having many hedonistic tendencies, regards suffering as unbearable.

For such people, the Stalinist terror was the most hated aspect of Communism, filling them with immense enmity against the regime. Their feelings were expressed in the mass escape of refugees, in messages smuggled out into the West, and even in revolutions. Their intense protest reached the Western World and made the Western observer conscious of labor camps and construction trials.

The new policy mitigates this hatred at its central source and removes the major psychological obstacle to these people's becoming Soviet men. Since the same policy is accompanied by a spectacular improvement in the standard of living, it creates a relatively favorable background for the imposition of the Red superego upon the satellite peoples. All these changes make the manipulative technique of Communism more effective than it ever was before, greatly reinforcing its effectiveness in the conquered countries where the resistance could be expected to be great. Altogether, the new policy greatly helps to realize Stalin's plan of exporting Communism and establishing Soviet countries beyond the borders of the Russian fatherland.

Yet, it would be foolish to believe that the past has been wiped off without any trace. The memories of the terror of yesteryear are still alive, and the new policy, with its inconsistencies and with its reluctance on the local level, still bears some resemblance to the policies of the past. Command and discipline are still at work, instilling into the subjects a certain feeling of the unknown guilt, inscribing the attitude of "forgive me" into their hearts, assigning them imperfections, sins and crimes. In a subtle way they still help to shape the Soviet man, making him amenable to the pariah psychology and the discipline of the party state. And this is, perhaps, what the opening story of this chapter means: under this system, the Soviet men suffer less psychological stress and those people who are alien to the Red superego suffer more. The plight of the faithful subject is alleviated by his faith, and it is the faithless who bear all the pains of the terror. However harsh or lenient the system may be, guilt and terror fit well into its general operation and strengthen the power of the regime.

IX. THE BELIEVERS

ONCE UPON A TIME (so one story goes) the party decided to clean out the bedbugs that infest the cities of Eastern Europe. It opened a sanitation drive and commanded all the citizens to exterminate the insect enemies within a fortnight. The campaign ended with a mass meeting at which everybody dutifully reported on his work. "My wife, myself, and the children," said the first citizen, "got down on our knees, scrubbed all woodwork with lye, burned the ironwork of the bed and plastered every crack in the wall. Thinking of last night, alas, I am afraid one bug is still left." "The store ran out of insecticide," spoke up the second citizen, "and did not expect a fresh supply before next spring." "We didn't do anything either," related the third, "because we have kept our place clean and haven't had any bugs." "We exterminated them," reported the fourth, "but new ones crawled over from the neighbor's apartment." There would have been more reports, but the party secretary, angered by such sloth, arose to scold his subjects. "None of you, comrades, has learned how to follow devotedly the instructions of our party. Now remember, if the party announces a housecleaning drive, it means that there must be bedbugs in every apartment, and whoever hasn't got them is an enemy of the people. But when the drive is over, no bedbugs must be left, and whoever has any then is an enemy of the people."

The humor here is really the broad farce of the old vaudeville stage, yet it aims at a crucial facet of Communism. Human nature is indeed a common stumbling block for social systems that are planned to be perfect; it is the treacherous reef upon which fanciful Utopias suffer shipwreck. The Utopian planners of a perfect future take it for granted that if a "good" plan is announced, humanity will necessarily adopt it. In a similar vein, Communism assumes that once a slogan, instruction, or order is issued, everybody will respond to it uniformly and act in harmony with the official prescriptions. But, human nature being what it is, man will respond to a norm of the superego or an instruction of the party in his own way. Every value evokes individual reactions, and the world of reality is always separate from the world of value. Neither the freedom of spontaneity nor the fear of vigorous sanctions makes men behave in complete uniformity. The citizens of the Red empire also react individually to the superego—accept or deny, realize or sabotage it. Their reactions are diverse, but in final analysis they determine the strength or weakness of Communism.

I

The two sides of a coin differ in design but are the same in denomination; it does not matter which side is seen. But the two sides of a collective superego—the demand and the acceptance—never represent the same amount. In the case of Communism, the party state clearly announces its demands, but it would be a gross mistake to confuse the demanded behavior with the actual behavior of the citizens. In spite of persuasion and terror, the citizen may reject a demand, and he accepts it only when his individual superego approves of it and when his loyalty is not dedicated to another collective superego.

A large and complex society (that of the Sovet Union as well as that of the United States) contains many religious, ethnic, regional, and occupational groups professing distinct sets of norms. Where many competing superegos are present, some arrangement must be made to regulate their coexistence and keep peace among them. One possible arrangement is freedom of conscience, a characteristic principle of Western civilization. It permits the existence of an unlimited number of superegos, gives them equal freedom to compete and proselyte, and allows the individual freedom to select among them. This is the basic principle of the American creed, which unites under its freedom such contradictory values as pro-Negro and anti-Negro attitudes, fundamentalism and free thought, the concepts of Senators La Follette and McCarthy. As another possible arrangement, the political power may step in to regulate the freedom of creeds and grant monopoly to one of them at the expense of the others. Freedom rules only a few societies, and monopolistic practices are more numerous. History names ancient Egypt, timeless India, and walled-in China as societies that sustained monopoly for astonishingly long times.

In modern Europe, Czarist Russia is the best example. Her monopolistic superego was born out of the lasting union of Czardom and the Orthodox Church. Early in the sixteenth century, the monk Philotheos addressed Grand Prince Basil III as "the only Czar for Christians in the whole world" and expounded the belief that after the fall of faithless Old Rome, after the fall of decadent Constantinople, Moscow had become the Third Rome—the strong and divine capital city of the orthodox faith and empire destined together to rule forever. Somewhat later, in the era of Ivan the Terrible, faithful service to the "Holy Russian Empire" was considered man's greatest merit. In time, the twin ideas were merged and elaborated by the Slavophile philosophy that captured Russia in the last century, about the same time that liberalism conquered Western Europe. The Slavophiles beheld Russia as the fullest and purest expression of Christianity and her people as "not a people [but] humanity." They believed that "Russian thought has found its incarnation" in the person of the Czar. Under his leadership, a great mission awaited Russia: to announce the truth of faith to the decaying, faithless West. Every subject had to identify himself with the crowned ruler, and Pogodin, writing in 1837, rendered the following homage to the Czarist superman: "All the physical and spiritual forces [of Russia] form a gigantic machine, constructed in a simple, purposeful way, directed by the hand of one single man, the Russian Czar, who with one motion can start it at any moment, who can give it any direction, any speed he wishes. . . . This machine is animated by one feeling, an ancient legacy from our ancestors: allegiance, limitless confidence, and devotion to the Czar, the God on earth."[1]

It is seldom possible to test the popularity of a superego by votes and statistics. However, one folk custom, the display of holy icons and the picture of the Czar in peasant homes, gives testimony of how widely the ideas of Holy Russia had penetrated the masses. To be sure, the ideas were supported by the popular customs of the Orthodox church and enforced by the terror of Czarism. All other beliefs were persecuted, and the Mennonites, Doukhobors, and Jews had to flee to America. A strict censorship excluded all the contaminating ideas of the West and earned international fame or infamy. A police system introduced brainwashing, made Dostoevsky mount the gallows only to pardon him at the last moment before execution—and the former revolutionary turned a staunch defender of the Third Rome.

When Czarism fell, some reformers hoped that conscience would be freed. As a sign of freedom, the revolution put the proletarian into the first-class railway carriage. He immediately tore off the velvet upholstery to make puttees out of it. Trotsky saw in the revolution "the awakening of the personality" in Ivan.[2] Ivan might very well have started to unfold his personality, but soon Communism established itself and found the practices of Czarism congenial and available. It adopted the Czarist heritage for its own use.

The old monopolistic superego was succeeded by a new one, and the succession did not require great change but only the transference of loyalty from one political system to another. The Czarist references were replaced by references to Bolshevism. The Czar's place on the side of the icons was taken by Lenin's picture. The Third International was substituted for the Third Rome; the capitalistic West, for the faithless West; service to the party, for service to Holy Russia. The two monopolistic superegos of Russian design had, almost like a father and a son, many common features. True, Communism has been unable to enlist the full support of folk customs, but it has made up for this failure by utilizing propaganda and command. With their aid, the monopolistic superego was strengthened and expanded. It was imposed upon the nomadic herdsmen of Inner Asia, hitherto undisturbed in their ancestral tribal life. In World War II, it was carried beyond the boundaries of the Soviet Union and forced upon the defeated peoples. Moscow and St. Petersburg have followed the same policy and have demanded the same submission of the masses before the official beliefs.

This is the historical background that shaped the demands of the Communist creed. From this point of view, it is of no importance that the satellite peoples (with the exception of the Germans) were opposed to the idea of the state's having a monopoly over matters of faith. The plan of Moscow called for the establishment of the Communist creed as the sole and general belief of all Soviet countries. The citizen, whatever his country of birth, had to fit himself into the framework of the total plan.

Wherever a monopolistic superego rules, every man must

take his stand. He cannot avoid facing the problem, although he can avoid the acceptance of the official belief. The choice among the possibilities is not always a matter of consciousness but always a matter of conscience. One may accept or refuse the official principles under the guidance of inner needs, desires, experiences, and do so without conscious deliberation; but one can enjoy peace of mind only when the accepted belief and one's individual superego are in good agreement. There are four choices that man can make in relation to a collective superego, and accordingly, there are four human types, each of them characterized by a different stand on the official beliefs.

The *faithful believer* makes the official belief a part of his individual superego, identifies himself sincerely, realizes the demands, and enjoys the blessings of a clear conscience.

The *lukewarm or halfhearted believer* does not fully internalize the collective belief, fails to realize the principles perfectly, and, perceiving his own weakness, struggles with his conscience.

The *opportunist* has no faith and does not make the principles a part of himself but feigns devotion and, with strains on his conscience, tries to comply outwardly with the belief.

The *faithless type* does not endeavor to comply with the official beliefs and does not find satisfaction in them but tries to go his own way.

II

The faithful Communist, the good and loyal comrade, the paragon of virtues and the hero of novels, is not so common as the official propaganda would have us believe. On the other hand, it would be equally fallacious to contend that the party finds no real support in the subjected masses. There cannot be much doubt that the party has its share of hard-core members who approach the official image of perfection rather well and work with sincere loyalty. Whether in a post of leadership or in a subordinate job, the faithful Communist firmly rejects all other creeds, dedicates all his efforts to the party, and is ready to sacrifice himself and everything that is dear to him for the cause. He attaches utmost importance to the party and relegates anything else to an inferior place. He has a one-track mind, refers everything to the movement, and evaluates everything by its bearing upon the movement. He demolishes any partition between the party and self and regards the two as one and the same. With this truly perfect identification, he is the fanatic.

In Communist society the fanatic enjoys a great psychological security, but he is ill at ease with free-thinkers and non-believers. This insecurity is repeatedly observed when Soviet officials, visiting a Western country, are confronted by inquisitive newsmen or by ordinary citizens of a capitalistic society. Small wonder that Communist believers—in the U.S. as well as in any Soviet country—tend to stick together, restrict their social life to the company of other believers, and spend their hours of work and leisure with people of their own kind. As one informant put it, "The friend of the party member is the next-door party member."

Anglo-Saxon societies, with their time-honored ideals of tolerance, broadmindedness, and moderation, consider the fanatic repugnant. Yet, they tolerate fanatics and raise them at certain times into important roles of social and political leadership. Communist society has very likely more fanatics and gives them the most important posts of leadership. Since chance alone does not produce fanatics, their abundance must be explained by the dynamics of Communism.

Like a huge suction pump, the party draws in all kinds of people but ejects the majority and keeps only the selected ones. It culls the incomers and subjects them to tests of loyalty and devotion. Those who fail are dropped; those who pass take their full course in the school of fanaticism, are formed, influenced, and strengthened in their belief till, in due time, they reach the degree of perfect identification. Only those can be molded who have the disposition to develop into good Communists and are willing to accept everything that is in store for them.

Man gives his loyalty to a group if it satisfies his needs for social relationships. A group that satisfies more needs more completely commands greater loyalty. Someone who has a great need of one group pays any price to gain admittance and submits himself to any demand. A juvenile may steal from his father and distribute the loot among the members of his gang because he desires the prestige that the gang allots for his deed. A highly complex organization such as the Communist party can satisfy a great many needs. It attracts people of various personality types and different needs who hope to receive some satisfaction through their membership and who pay the admittance fee, in work and self-sacrifice, according to the intensity of their needs.

One pressing need is to find a collective superego. The individual is not self-sufficient; he requires a creed that he can share with his fellow beings and that serves as the framework of social interactions. The collective superego contains the goals and values common in a group and, through them, regulates co-operation and competition. People co-operate and compete because they all are in pursuit of the same highly rated group value.

Man usually absorbs the collective superego of his primary group, of his family and community. He absorbs it as a natural process during the formative years of his personality development, when he is most exposed to it. Exposure generally leads to identification, and a more intense exposure (or the relative absence of competing superegos), to a stronger identification. The intense and long-lasting exposure given in the family home is a powerful force that transmits the same norms and values to successive generations. Man's identification is usually fixed by the time he reaches maturity, establishes a family, and takes his place as a full-fledged member of society.

This process, however, is oftentimes halted and delayed. Some people may be unable to fix their identification, may fail to absorb it in the home or actually may reject the parental superego. Having passed the usual age of maturity, they still lack norms they can accept as regulators of their actions. With dissatisfaction and indecision in their hearts, they search for a person, ideology, or other object of identification. These restless searchers are common in any group. Literature has commemorated some eternal figures of this sort—the intellectual Dr. Faustus, the indecisive Prince Hamlet, the cynical J. Alfred Prufrock, the aristocratic Pierre Bezuhov, the mystic Aloysha Karamazov.

Acceptance of a superego is partly chance and partly choice. It is a work of chance in so far as it depends on complex and unpredicable circumstances which are beyond the control of the individual. It is a work of choice in so far as it is a selection among several possibilities. Any decision involving choice—the purchase of a home by a family, the artistic selection of words by a writer, or the finding of a superego by a searching soul—has its own detailed motivation. I can discern ten important motives that explain why a person chooses Communism, and a detailed discussion of these motives is necessary to understand the attractive power of the party. After all, the party does attract many people from all walks of life.

Nowadays, the Communist superego lives as a tradition in many homes of the Soviet countries and also of the proletarian neighborhoods in Western Europe. Thus, it can be absorbed in a natural way during youth, and this is the first motive of attraction to the party. As the saying goes, "The children of big Communists turn out to be even bigger Communists." In France and Italy one may hear of "third-generation Communists," who have grown up in that belief since the inception of the party. In Hungary, although the party was outlawed from 1919 to 1945, many potential Communists still transferred their ideas to the children. Twenty-year old László Kotró, executed for his party membership in 1944, wrote in a last letter to his parents, "You should be consoled to know that I am going to my death with courage. I have become stronger and believe daddy's words even more."[3]

And this is the long-range aim of the party policy: to turn every family home into a school of Communism, to entrust a "revolutionary goal" to women, to establish the "Communist spirit in the family."[4] The policy is pursued with vigor and tenacity and brings forth results. One can expect that with every passing year more homes will be penetrated by the Red superego and more "born Communists" will swell the ranks of the believers.

One may or may not accept Sigmund Freud's theory on the role that the father image plays in developing a superego. There cannot be, however, much doubt that paternal authority often becomes a symbol of norms and values. Thus, any revolt against parental authority (rather common in our civilization) may lead to denying the norms and values of the home. In the conflict of generations, the sons often become "nihilists"—to use the word coined by Turgenev—and discard the values of the fathers. They may do it in a shocking way, and the examples of *enfants terribles* are numerous: rebelling children of hard-working, profit-hungry bourgeois end up as playboys, bohemians, or Communists. A domestic rebel may deny his father and everything for which the father stands. He may attempt to destroy the person of the father and everything that makes that person, for example, the capitalistic order. His hatred of his father can be projected into the social order, and the young scion of a bourgeois family may sincerely believe that he has been wronged by capitalism. In this rebellion is the second motivation I discern.

This domestic revolt has driven into the movement people of middle-class origin, of whom Lenin is one example. Among the lesser figures of Communism, one encounters the son of a bank director revolting against the liaison of his father with a girl not older than the son himself; another youngster provided with all the comfort of a bourgeois home but hating the social climbing of his *nouveau riche* father, a feather merchant; or the very obese girl who holds her parents responsible for her sexual maladjustment.[5] Small wonder that many who received a religious education at home turned Communist. Seminarians had an important part in the Russian revolutionary movements, Stalin being one of them; one survey found that the majority of Western Communists came from homes with a strong religious background.[6]

The rebel is a frequent enough type, but his counterpart is just as common. The dependent individual, who is impelled by the third kind of motivation, is unable to loosen his parental ties when the due time comes and needs parental authority even beyond the normal age of maturation. He looks for a substitute when paternal guidance is missing and readily submits to any strong-willed person or institution. Since this attitude is important in establishing the authority of the various forms of leadership, social life offers many approved ways of finding a substitute. Females are encouraged to find one in a husband, males, in a political or social leader. Old autocrats usually assumed a fatherly pose before their subjects, and even politicians in the democracies judge it useful to employ this device.

As Communism established itself in power, it replaced the fatherly pose of the Czar with that of the powerful Red leaders. The name of "father" was given to Lenin, Stalin, and some of the lesser leaders, and through them the party itself came to be regarded as a father substitute: a stern, wrathful, inclement father who still lays claim upon the affections of all. One party functionary was described as quoting alternately the slogans of the party and the dicta of his father. Another one characterized himself by saying, "I was an orphan, and the party reared me."

These statements should not be dismissed as empty rhetoric. Devoted Communists submit to the authority of the party as obediently as the child to the words of his father. Filial submission is a characteristic mark of the good Communist and shows up at those crucial times when the party executes a sudden change in policy. When Moscow ordered the American Communist Party to purge Earl Browder from leadership, the members immediately yielded to the orders, and those persons attacked the fallen leader most vehemently who had been closely associated with him and had been dubbed "Browder's boys" and described as being "fastened to Browder's mental apron-strings."[7]

Not every superego derives from the parental home. People may formulate norms and values quite independently, under the impact of their own experiences. The independent spirits (as they are often called) represent various philosophical tenets, one type of which deserves special attention—idealism. The superego of the idealist is of his own creation, altruistic, bent upon the welfare of mankind, pondering great reforms and preaching self-sacrifice. But, as it happens, the idealist is often doomed to loneliness. His ideas are not shared by his fellow citizens and cannot be realized in society at large. He may respond to this rejection with a proud, voluntary withdrawal from the community as the literary heroes of Henrik Ibsen did. As another frequent response, the idealist may look for the support of a small group, being led to this exploration by the fourth kind of motivation.

The searching idealist is particularly common among intellectuals and semi-intellectuals who often set out on an erratic journey to some noble goal. On one leg of the erratic journey, the idealist may arrive in the Communist party which, in the misleading light of enthusiasm, may seem sympathetic to his own ideals. Communism, however, does not permit deviations, and the searching idealist sooner or later has to realize that he desires something other than the party gives. Now, misplaced idealism will be his predicament. He may either surrender to the party or lose his illusions—a bitter experience for the lonely idealist. Disillusionment has many solutions, but idealists often take the most extreme recourse, the flight from the world of their lost illusions. Famed poets, painters, actors, disappointed in Communism, chose suicide.

For the idealist the party may be a tragic disappointment, but for many of the common breed the party holds out the promise of satisfying the need for intellectual security (this promise is the fifth motivation). Man is generally eager to know, desires the knowledge that will bring order into a confusing and self-contradictory world. Communism claims to have the correct answers, and there are many who wish to share this infallible knowledge. Half-educated people are the regular dupes of charlatan philosophies, and they furnish a common type of Communist: the party functionary with modest schooling who can retort to every question with an appropriate slogan. But men of learning and men of power also look to the party to find intellectual security. A poet did find it there and felt relieved: "As simple was the logic of our fate," he remembered, "as the choice between honor and vile treason, between water and fire, between life and death." As a testimony coming from quite a different environment, Stewart Alsop recalled his undergraduate days at Yale in similar terms: "It was the supreme logic of Marxism which made everything in contemporary history so luminously clear. . . . It [did] your thinking for you." As a practical example of the same case, the old war hero, Frunze, hesitated to undergo a serious surgical operation but submitted himself to the doctor's scalpel when ordered to do so by the Politbureau.[8]

A superego, moreover, gives emotional and social security (the sixth motivation) by banding together the believers into small groups and uniting them in faith and work. There the believer finds companions of his kind with whom he can work for common goals, relax in his spare time, share ideas and sentiments, and establish sincere intimacy. Everybody wants to belong somewhere, and the tightly knit group of a party cell promises camaraderie, friendly relations, understanding, close human ties that cannot be established otherwise. As the official press has it, the comrades surround the unfortunate and lonely ones with "the warmth and heat of the most spiritual human flame, love"; and nothing but loyalty to the cause is necessary to gain that companionship.[9]

Those who lack social relationships ardently hope that the party will solve their problems of loneliness and isolation. Those who are devoid of social graces, who are shy and withdrawing, who are the unattractive outcasts of social life, join the movement in earnest dedication. Rootless, marginal people who do not seem to belong anywhere are always sensitive targets of Communist propaganda, the immigrants in America just as well as the migrants to the cities of Soviet countries. As a further, tragic example, one could cite the case of the deaf-mutes in Hungary. In 1945, the leadership of their national organization and a great many members joined the Communist movement as a body.

Camaraderie is, in itself, a consolation in times of sorrow and vicissitude. In addition, the superegos offer bountiful rewards to the faithful. In particular, they offer specific recompenses for the sufferings and deprivations of life. They hold out a return for distress, promise generous and appealing prizes to give meaning to work and suffering. The creed with a more general relief and a more sympathetic consolation has a stronger hold and may appeal to all the "insulted and injured."

Communism proclaims itself the archenemy of capitalism and appeals to all who have been insulted and injured by the social order (the seventh motivation). Its appeal is very broad, since any personal frustration can be projected into the outside world and attributed to the existing economic system. Capitalism can be made the scapegoat for sufferings which are not necessarily connected with the prevailing mode of production. This is the usual formula of Communist propaganda, which indicts capitalism as often as possible on every account. It attributes the melancholy poetry of Pushkin to the gross inequities of the economic order and blames Wall Street for any present-day shortcoming in the Soviet Union. It reminds the audience time and time again that the party is the sole instrument that compensates for deprivations and remedies wrongs.

The propaganda has paid off handsomely; the motif of deprivation has worked miracles. Poverty, ignorance, and persecution have been the best agitators for Communism, converting entire groups, the proletarian class of Europe, with its traditional radical inclinations, being a classical example. Persecution made the Jews (and some other minority groups as well) susceptible to Communism. The Bolshevik party of Russia triumphed in 1917 with the help of the most deprived elements of the population. The soldiers and sailors, writhing under the torments of three ravaging war years, rallied around the flag of Trotsky and Lenin and gave momentum to an obscure leftist party.

Individual deprivation has made its own contribution to Communist membership. "Oh, my friends, I have not eaten for seven days," sighed the nineteen-year-old poet, and presently he joined the party.[10] The woman just passing through the menopause, the much-bullied youngest son of a family of seven, the social outcast of the East European village, all looked for their own specific relief in the same organization. Dissatisfaction may spur anybody to comply with the Red norms, and a maladjusted person may find amidst the moil and toil of party work his psychological equilibrium.

Every superego is ready to perpetuate and defend itself. It fights anything that threatens its existence and obliges the believers to participate in the fight. In other words, it designates permissible targets of aggression, although it prohibits aggression against certain other targets; it labels attack against designated targets as a praiseworthy duty, but regards attack against other designated targets as a punishable sin. Certain superegos are aggressive, specify many targets, and recommend the use of violence. Others are peaceful, restricting hostility or altogether banning the use of physical force.

The American creed advocates a practical peacefulness and tries to remove the targets of aggression through tolerance, co-operation, and amicable settlement of conflicts. The Communist superego, on the other hand, is aggressive. If there were no other indications, the press attests to this difference. An issue of the *New York Times* selected at random contained only one article naming a hostile group (which happened to be the Communist party) but printed four articles pleading for tolerance and compromise. The central organ of the Hungarian Communist Party, in its issue of the same date, published six aggressive items and named seventeen groups as enemies; it recommended "relentless fight," "eradication," and "liquidation" six times altogether.

Communism releases the militancy of the believer. It permits him to select the targets of his personal aggression out of the many evil enemies of the Red demonology. He can assail not only distant persons and abstract institutions, such as the capitalists and Wall Street, but also workmates, neighbors, rivals, and other nearby "enemies of the people." Personal aggressiveness reserves a greater fury for neighbors, and its greatest rage is for rivals. Thus, the party satisfies the aggressive tendencies of many and turns personal struggle into a characteristic feature of the regime. To add fuel to the fire, it allows not only verbal aggression but also direct action. An anonymous denunciation of a neighbor, a mass demonstration against imperialists and kulaks, may give as much satisfaction as a successful physical attack. The party functionary who bullies the subjects under his jurisdiction, the journalist who pens a vitriolic attack, the little clerk who scribbles in one of the personal files in a cadre department, may satisfy perfectly all his aggressive needs in his own way. This satisfaction of aggression is the eighth motivation.

The party lures the aggressive people, and this is one reason why it attracts the males rather than the females, the young rather than the old people. It puts them all under iron discipline and channels their attack against the official enemies. It specifies targets that must be attacked on order but severely punishes any unauthorized aggression. The American Communist Party expelled those who deviated from the rules and, at the same time, pressured its followers into militant but fruitless strikes. In a proclamation it called upon the New York transit workers in these words: "You must direct your strikes against the government and must overthrow the capitalist government. When the final struggle to overthrow the government comes you must have guns in your hands."[11] The guns, of course, must be used according to the orders of the party. The member must not live out his own aggression but may receive vicarious gratification. The good Communist, when attacking the targets designated by the party, takes them as substitutes for enemies of his own choice. During a mass demonstration, when the effigy of Tito was lynched and burned, one participant exclaimed, "Treat him as if he were your boss!"

Recalcitrant members whose actual aggression cannot be canalized are dropped. Those, however, who can manipulate their aggression within the bounds of the official plans are rewarded, often with the highest posts. The upper cadre opens to those people who skillfully defeat their rivals and emerge successfully from the personal struggles, who fight the targets of the party as if they were their own and do not infringe upon the taboos. Aggressiveness is a characteristic mark of Red leadership, and it insures that the character of Communist policy will remain basically aggressive.

The superego, by its very essence, inflates self-confidence. Any believer (and any member of a powerful organization) feels his inner powers increased. The Communist party bolsters the self-confidence of its members as a matter of policy, and it is not modest about its virtues. The party claims to be the élite of the working class, the vanguard of the revolutionary forces, a group that is select, professional, and unique in character. It makes the member believe that he is a part of a world-wide movement, that he has a special vocation to work for Messianic aims, to perform momentous deeds and to change the course of history. If anything more is needed, then the regular operation of the movement furnishes it. For example, the youngster of the Komsomol, singing with his group, "We climb up into heaven and drive out all the gods," may feel in himself the

strength of superhuman powers.[12] This self-confidence is the ninth ground of attraction to the party.

Communist self-confidence, so often manifested at critical times, is the result of an intricate psychological process. The member has faith in the party because it gratifies his needs and faith in himself because of his identification with the party. He injects the self-assurance of the party into his self and regards himself as strong; at the same time, he projects his personal gratification into the party and regards it as omnipotent. One believer thought that the party was capable of anything, even of "the indefinite postponement of death." And he continued: "To travel from the capitalist world into Soviet territory is to pass from death to birth."[13]

The injection and projection strengthen each other like the double cables of a moored boat. The boat is tossed but securely fastened; self-confidence is rocked by vicissitudes but not wrecked. On the contrary, it is increased by every act of duty and by every reward received for faithfulness. The good Communist cannot feel humiliated while fighting and suffering for the party; the very injustice inflicted by the party adds to his pride and self-respect. Under any pressure and stress he is self-assured as a Communist, although he may be undecided and doubting as a private man. Self-confidence is a product of faith; the leaders, then, possess a greater amount of both. They possess that blind determination that characterizes the whole regime. A democracy may promote doubting, self-probing personalities to leadership, but Bolshevism advances the grimly determined, undoubting fanatics. Their leadership ensures the uncompromising radicalism of the Communist parties.

In this way the party attracts all kinds of people. Inferiority feelings can be compensated (and also overcompensated), ambitions realized, and high goals of aspiration achieved through loyalty to the party. In the Communist countries only the party members have a chance to satisfy their ambitions. In the capitalistic countries those who are unable to find other outlets for their ambitions may become Communists. This was, according to one witness, what happened in the case of William Z. Foster, a fallen and forsaken labor leader after the steel strike of 1920, who beheld the party as the only road to leadership and authority.[14]

A penetrating study of defected Communists in the Western countries found that neurotic needs had motivated many to join the party; and neurotic motivation is stronger in the middle class than in the working class, stronger in the United States and England (where Communism appeals only to a deviant minority) than in France and Italy (where Communism is traditionally accepted by a large segment of the population).[15] The Western observer finds it logical indeed to probe for neurotic tendencies when he sees a strong identification with a queer, enslaving creed. His suspicion, however, does not seem to be corroborated by the evidence coming from Communist-dominated countries.

Identification with Communism is, in itself, a complex but "normal" process. A person joins the party because through this act he expects to satisfy certain personal needs. This expectation, however, seldom rises to the level of consciousness, and he is unaware of his real motivation. He is willing to project his motive into the outer world and to believe that there is some objective, rational foundation for his becoming a Communist. He is all too satisfied to accept the party's official explanation that he joined because of his conviction that the capitalistic world is wrong and the Soviet world right. He is willing to repress his real involvement and to satisfy his real needs not openly but under the guise of carrying out the regular duties of the party. This repression of actual needs is a necessary condition of perfect identification—a serious and difficult but "normal" process.

On the other hand, there cannot be much doubt that the belligerent organization of Communism attracts some neurotics and that the neurotic motivation should be the tenth in our list. The poet Attila József expressed his motivation in these words: "The party is lovely, colorful, lively and natural like a luscious peach on the tree. The sight of peaches brings the image of the party to my mind." As the affectionate symbolism suggests, a neurotic who has no other love object may concentrate his tender emotions upon the party and may gain an almost sexual satisfaction from his relationship with the Communist movement. But whatever his specific motivation, the neurotic finds it hard to get into the party and even harder to stay there. Communism does not stand for aberrations. The neurotic, if admitted, will not tolerate the strict discipline, the heavy work load, and the psychological strains of identification. He will be a transient in the party, soon either being purged or leaving voluntarily, with bitterness and a loss of faith. Attila József renounced his faith amidst loud cries of "Plague upon the party!" and rewrote his propaganda-inspired poetry.

Altogether, it seems that neurotic motivation may be important in those countries where Communists make up a small, deviant minority and are moved to a general protest against the ruling norms and values. However, where Communism is an accepted system, neurosis cannot be more common among party members than in comparable segments of the total population. As a particular point, there is no reliable evidence that abnormal psychological traits are prevalent in the highly selected group of Red leaders. Neurotics are to be found in Communist countries, but they do not cluster within the party; they are apt to find their place in quite a different area of Bolshevik society.

The ten motives cited above have produced many faithful Communists. But motives are, after all, theoretical abstractions that do not appear in pure form. In real life it is always an individual combination of several motives, character traits, and social conditions that makes a good Communist. The possible combinations (such as ambition and long exposure to the party, youth and loneliness, aggressiveness and deprivation) make a long and tedious list. In the case of Lenin, for example, the original rebellion against the paternal authority was followed by other memorable experiences: the execution of his brother, the social boycott suffered in his home town, other deprivations, and literary influences. These, together with his needs for security and dominance, added up to an exceptionally strong motivation that drove him all his life.[16]

Each Communist has his own motivation. He is an individuum, with all those unique traits which distinguish one man from another; it is a great fallacy (committed all too frequently in the Western World) to apply stereotypes to party members. The hard-core Communists show a great diversity of human characteristics and have, in fact, only one characteristic in common: they derive sincere satisfaction from loyalty and service to the cause. They are attached to the movement by that satisfaction and not by rational considerations. Their faith in the Red superego cannot be shaken by argument or evidence. They fulfill their duties with the peace of mind attendant upon a good conscience. Their brand of felicity, however, is not enviable.

III

Not every party member is a good Communist. The official parlance often speaks of "lukewarm," "irresolute," or "halfhearted" Communists, who are weak in their belief, harbor certain doubts, and fall short of the exacting requirements.[17] In motives they are similar to the good Communists; they are neither corrupt nor deceptive, just weaker in support of the burden that the party puts upon believers. Hence, the "irresolute" member cannot absolutely reject the other creeds; the "lukewarm" Communist questions some tenets and does not regard the word of the leaders as the truth; and his "halfhearted" comrade tries featherbedding in party work, gives a substandard performance, misses a meeting, or puts aside an unpleasant instruction.

The halfhearted believer is a frequent type among the followers of the Red superego, yet his portrait cannot be drawn easily. He has two different faces, according to the angle from which we view him. If we compare him to the fanatic, a picture of weakness, imperfection, and other negative traits appears. In this comparison he emerges as the man who dedicates not the "whole of his life" but only a part of it to the cause. Yet he has some faith, suffers for his faults, and is tormented by a conscience that (however tardy and hesitant) still lives in a weak character like his. With his repeated lapses, his remorse, and his decisions to improve himself, he is a social type very similar to the alcoholic in America.

He is a weakling and a believer at the same time and can perform many useful roles for the regime. He accepts the subordinate, thankless posts and does passable work. The functionary in a tractor station in the remote countryside may be a philanderer, a loafer, a braggart, or a sulk, may be ignorant of the labor theory of value, but may still be usable in his job. The remorse-ridden, irresolute Communist is, in particular, the whipping boy of the system, blamed and punished for any shortcomings, for those of his own and those of others. If the party requires self-criticism, he may testify about his own crimes and other people's crimes. If the police need an obedient tool, he may act as an effective denunciator, an obvious figure in the purges, a conspicuous victim in construction trials, always ready to accuse himself and others. The system that depends upon the uneasy conscience that does not remember the source of its guilt could not be maintained without the halfhearted believers. That system needs not only potential criminals but also potential victims who can collaborate in their own immolation.

In order to see the other face of the halfhearted man, we have to compare him to the rest of the population, to the even less perfect and ideologically even more backward citizens. Now we behold the picture of the comrade who under the guidance of the party has greatly advanced from his original imperfect state, has improved himself, and has reached an advanced level of perfection. Now we behold what Communist faith can produce even in a weak character, and this product is worthy of being shown to the general public. One case in point is the mother of seven children who works in a pharmaceutical company and overfulfills her production norm by 130 per cent, keeps the home spick-and-span, and (with the help of her husband) brings up a healthy, well-fed, well-clad, and hard-working family. Her shortcomings are those that can be expected in working-class surroundings: a lack of higher aspirations and a neglect of education. Yet, with all her shortcomings she is still an exemplary citizen, attractively portrayed in a national magazine for women.[18]

The party operates as a school for fanatics but knows that only those people can be made fanatics who have a specific predisposition. The production of halfhearted believers is an easier task and yields Soviet men who, in spite of their shortcomings, are amenable to manipulation and respond to official command and persuasion. Hence, the halfhearted believer must have a place within the party, a place that is determined by the general policy of the regime. Stalinism, with its insistence upon true and fanatic belief, was greatly angered by the shortcomings of lukewarm Communists, treated them harshly, and vented its wrath in the frequent purges. The policy of Khrushchev looked at the same type of believer from a different angle and discovered his positive qualities. The new policy allots a more stable and secure place to the halfhearted type and, by doing so, has increased the proportion of the halfhearted among the party members, an increase that has occurred at the expense of the opportunists.

The Stalinist policy, to be sure, followed the line of Russian tradition, which had assigned to the fanatic a prominent place of leadership in the Czarist court and in religion, as well as in revolutionary movements. The new policy does not necessarily mean a sharp break with the past, but it does signal an important innovation that appeals to some of the satellite peoples. Hungarian or Czech culture, for example, has never favored fanaticism, and the citizen reared in those cultures is more likely to become a halfhearted than a full believer. The current policy makes the demands of Communism more acceptable to these people and, by recruiting from among them enough halfhearted comrades, creates a conspicuous, exemplary group of citizens who have been formed and shaped by the manipulative practices of the party, have progressed toward the officially prescribed goals, and attest the success of Communist man-making.

IV

Reliable witnesses claim that many party members are neither faithful believers nor halfhearted believers but "careerists" or opportunists. The faithful believer joins the party because of his non-conscious need, the opportunist because of rational consideration and a calculated hope for advantage. The latter signs up in hope of gaining success and furthering his career. He has no serious conviction but feigns a loyalty. In the depths of his heart, he is not attached to the demanding and harassing superego and is prone to leave the party whenever it is to his advantage to do so. However, as long as he is bound by his considered interest he tries to comply with the requirements in every outward sign and thereby to earn the praise of his superiors.

Milovan Djilas is not the only one who has alleged that almost the whole party membership consists of opportunists.[19] Other sources, however, have put the number of "good Communists" higher. Our Hungarian informants gave various estimates, claiming that 5 to 33 per cent of the members were faithful; 1 to 10 per cent, halfhearted; and the rest, opportunists. Their estimates represent crude guesswork and have no numerical significance; they are, however, what public opinion believes the figures to be. The public knows that whoever desires success has to join the party. And indeed, party members figure conspicuously in occupations with great prestige and a high standard of living. At one time, only 3 per cent of the citizens of the U.S.S.R. were party members, but 20 per cent of the doctors, 38 per cent of the engineers, and 86 per cent of the army officers and generals were members either of the party or of the Komsomol. In East Germany, where teaching enjoys the prestige of old, 60 per cent of all teachers belong to the party.[20]

The total number of opportunists is actually greater than these figures would indicate. It includes a great many fellow travelers, functionaries of mass organizations, and holders of important jobs who, although not members, regularly co-operate with the party. This large mass of opportunists furnishes those corrupt officials whose misdeeds are frequently noted in the press, the culprits who become "separated from the masses" and "lose touch with reality," who put their own advantage above that of the party and get involved in graft, bribery, and embezzlement. Officialdom fights them relentlessly and metes out severe punishments but has not yet made headway against their eternal presence. In view of the thorough cadre and police screening given party members, it is astonishing that official spokesmen repeatedly complain that people with criminal records turn up as members, and even functionaries, of the party.

The loud complaints, however, should not mislead us. Not every opportunist is corrupt in the legal sense of the word. Most of them never trespass into forbidden territory but serve with seeming faith and real usefulness. Being ambitious and efficient workers, often having great skills and unusual intelligence, they play important roles in every large-scale organization—government, army, or business. They can be found in every branch of Communist administration, in many posts of power and authority. They may feign so well that they deceive the cadre department itself; more often, however, their frame of mind is known but they are tolerated for their services. A factory manager, for example, in his past and present positions was known to engage in "profiteering," establishing a small farm on the land belonging to the factory, selling the produce, and pocketing the income. Yet his superiors in the national industrial management overlooked all complaints because of his "excellent managerial abilities." And indeed, he was able to establish and build up a factory with 200 workers "without any investment" in less than eight months.[21]

It is a hard lot indeed to feign loyalty since doing so necessitates endless lying in every matter. In addition, the opportunist does not derive gratification from party work but finds it distasteful and humiliating. Nevertheless, he shoulders the heavy burdens in order to receive something he desires: promotion, success, power, or an easy life. The state of his conscience depends on his personal luck. If he gets what he desires, he may enjoy peace of mind; if he fails in his personal aims, he may be tormented by dissatisfaction, tension, insecurity. But of all people, the opportunist is most likely to silence his discontent. Courage, resistance, and a sense of justice are not his virtues. However frustrated he may be in achieving the cherished goals of his ambition, he always possesses some little gain which he is unwilling to sacrifice; and in the defense of this present position, he will always go along with the party. This attitude is important when assessing the strength of the Communist regimes—many are the people who wish to preserve some small gain and are willing to go along.

X. PEOPLE IN THE COLD

KÁROLY, THE YOUNG STUDENT (as one informant told his story), desired nothing more than to leave behind the sedentary life of the university, volunteer for a kolkhoz, and contribute actively to the progress of Soviet agriculture. As soon as the authorities gave their permission, he boarded a train and, within a few hours, found himself at a village railway station. A lone old peasant from the kolkhoz greeted him, and the two of them set out for the farm. It was a bitter-cold winter day, and the two men laboriously trudged forward in the deep, fresh snow. Károly was bristling with questions about the kolkhoz, but his companion clamped down the lambskin cap on his ears and seemed to be deaf to any words. At last, they caught sight of a group of peasants clearing the road of snow, wielding heavy shovels, then pausing and warming their numb fingers with their breath. The old companion winked in their direction and remarked, "The members of the co-operative do their job in cold or heat." Then again the two of them walked along silently. Finally, the whitewashed houses of the kolkhoz, their chimneys smoking and their thatched roofs steaming, emerged from the desolate winter scenery. The two walkers hastened their steps, and presently they reached the kolkhoz. They entered the administration building and there, around a red-hot potbelly stove, they found a group of five, drinking tea and smoking pipes. "These are the members of the party," remarked the old peasant, "holding an important meeting. And this is life in the kolkhoz—a few Communists keeping warm around the stove, and the people working outside in the cold."

The fictional trip to the kolkhoz allegorically refers to life far beyond the confines of a snowbound village, to life anywhere in the country. The allegory suggests that whenever faithful Communists and skeptics meet, it is a meeting of drones and drudges. Certain facts, indeed, seem to uphold this view. In Soviet society, Communists make up a small élite. In the U.S.S.R., party members have never amounted to more than 4 per cent of the population, although in some satellite countries membership has risen as high as 10 per cent of all inhabitants. Even if one adds the former members (a considerable number after so many purges) and the various kinds of fellow travelers (consistent supporters of the regime), the total is still a minority. The bulk of the subjects (called "masses," "outsiders," and "enemies" in the Red hierarchy) are unable or unwilling to gather closely around the warm stove of the party. Our opening story calls them—appropriately—the people in the cold. The question that remains to be answered is: what makes them drudge?

I

That multitude shares certain common characteristics. Its members do not surrender their norms and values in favor of those of the party; they make attempts of various kinds to maintain their personal autonomy; they are not identified with the party and regard the world as a great dichotomy of "we versus Communism." Consequently, they are excluded from many privileges and benefits.

People in the cold cannot approve of the Red norms and cannot fit themselves into the framework of Bolshevism. Some of them may be strong and self-sufficient in their beliefs, in no need of a collective superego. Perhaps to this group belonged those Spanish Republicans who, in the opinion of one witness, were "individualists" and not Communists during their Civil War.[1] Most people, however, are less individualistic and self-sufficient and long for the guidance of a collective superego. One writer under Communist rule expressed their sentiment: "For eleven years, we have been thirsty for the true essence of human and national existence."[2] This thirst cannot be satisfied by a humanistic and nationalistic creed, but it is often quenched by a partial acceptance of the Red norms. And indeed, the constant propaganda reaches many people with Bolshevik philosophy and makes them accept one tenet although they deny another.

People in the cold have more or less repressed and silenced, hidden and unrealized individual superegos. Accordingly, they may stand anywhere: very far from, or rather near to, the Red norms. But wherever they stand, they are not believers. For them, Communism is a source of incessant frustration because it prohibits them from unfolding their individuality. They visualize themselves as drudges in the service of a few drones. To be sure, frustration is a regular part of human life which man, whatever the political or social climate into which his fate has cast him, cannot altogether avoid. However, he tries to cope with failure and find adequate recompense for every defeat suffered. Often he can do so by replacing his goals: if he is frustrated in one field, he may be able to find satisfaction elsewhere. The possibility of compensatory satisfaction greatly mitigates every frustration.

Communism, however, shuts off the usual outlets of compensatory satisfaction. People in the cold cannot amass fortunes or be successful in their occupations, they cannot "write out" their grievances or look for other consolations as they please. They are doomed to live with their frustrations. In this respect they are alike, but otherwise they constitute a motley army. It would be erroneous to think that all of them react in the same way and reject the Red superego in an identical and equal manner. Actually, they take their own attitudes to the regime, which may range anywhere from a slight sympathy, through neutralism and fence-sitting, to straight opposition and eventual resistance. Their reactions to Communism are as variegated as human nature and the given circumstances permit. But their reactions fall into five common types.

Compromise is the first. "It's not a must to become a hero; it may be impossible," said one poet, expressing a common-sense truth and a motto for many.[3] The person who selects the unheroic way of life accommodates himself to the existing conditions and chooses the attitude that is most bearable for him. He determines for himself how much he will render to Caesar and takes his stand, accordingly, somewhere between loyalty and resistance. He makes his compromise and looks for a relative security; takes the road of least resistance and gives the minimum loyalty that assures his personal safety. The compromise may be sincere and, again, it may be insincere. There are people who are indifferent towards creeds in general and make a practical compromise with ease. Then again, there are people who lead a life of duplicity, appearing as loyal subjects in public and taking off the mask in private. As one refugee reminisced, "Everybody was an actor. There were as many actors as citizens in the country, some of them talented, others just poor hams." Man may be able to deceive the authorities, but not himself. Conscience, in its own particular way, takes account of many things that the conscious self wishes to overlook. And whoever gains security through an insincere compromise has to pay for it with an uneasy conscience, with constant tensions and stresses which consume a great part of his inner energies.

The plan for creating the first generation of Soviet man, carried out in the U.S.S.R. between 1917 and 1945, called for producing relatively few believers but many sincere compromisers. The plan (so I think) basically succeeded, and at present the majority of the citizens have reconciled themselves with the Red superego and willingly comply with the demands made by the party state. The plan for making a second Soviet generation specified the same objectives, but it met with special difficulties. The majority of the satellite peoples were much opposed to Communism, and this resistance, deeply rooted in their national culture and psychology, could not be overcome within a short time.

As a result, the sincere compromisers are relatively few in the satellite countries, although their number increases with the passage of time, and the new policy of Khrushchev takes great pains to make this kind of compromise easy and popular. Nevertheless, the citizens of those countries are still likely to be insincere in their reconciliation and insecure in their adaptation to the regime. They are likely to react in negative ways to the political system.

Man naturally tries to resolve his tensions, but this is not always feasible for him. The subject of Communism who does not make his compromise is in any case powerless against the regime and cannot remove the real causes of his tension. He may try another solution: escape from what causes the tension; that is the second type of reaction. Whenever the stresses grow too heavy, he feels a great desire to free himself from anything that involves a Communist confession of faith and seizes any possible way of achieving this end, realistic or not.

The crudest form of escapism is to "bury one's head in the sand" and ignore the existing situation. An extreme case reported to me was that of an old man who elected to live as a hermit, refused to leave his apartment, and excluded newspapers, radio, and other messages from the outer world; he withdrew from the realities, and within a self-imposed confinement he led his own life, free of serious problems of conscience. Such a complete withdrawal is a luxury that few people can afford. The average man cannot turn his back on life but has to make a living and care for his family. He cannot bury his head in the sand, at least not for any length of time. Still, he tries to forget about the Red norms and thereby to gain a partial relief, a brief escape. One of my informants illustrated this attitude by recalling the well-known bric-a-brac representing three little monkeys who clamp their hands upon their eyes, ears, and mouths. Similarly, people do not wish to see, to hear, and to speak anything that refers to the official creed. They skip the political items in the newspapers but devour the sport pages; are aware of the horrors of the labor camps but do not talk of them; witness corruption and theft but do not seem to notice it.

As another form of escapism, one may take up any pleasant activity that, though it does not remove the tension, offers gratification in its own right. An intense, tender family life may be an escape just as well as a pleasant hobby: music, chess, sports or any fad that, in a sudden wave of popularity, acquires a multitude of fans. From time to time, as the Communist press notes in shocked tones, a "hysteria" sweeps across the masses, a hysteria of playing bridge, of seeking sexual adventures, of dancing, drinking, and even crime.

As a passive form of escapism, one may build up a dream world and retire there. Phantasies bestow all the pleasures that the real world denies; but if one wants to avoid the ridicule aimed at Don Quixote, one must hide his dreams before everybody except a few intimates. It may be argued with good reason that frustration makes people indulge in reveries and, consequently, that Bolshevism brings forth castle-builders. Whatever the case may be, a fascinating dream emerges before those who shiver in the cold: liberation from Red rule, the characteristic dream of satellite peoples.

In the Soviet Union, where the majority are willing to

accept and support the regime, few are those who think of "liberation." In the countries of the second generation, however, the idea of a non-Communist system is still much alive, although its realization is known to be beyond the power of those who desire it. People who see the internal strength of the regime and their own impotence hope for a miraculous change, which would occur suddenly, through a fortunate political turn, revolution or war. Their dreams are intimately linked to international affairs. The dreamers follow the news of world politics with an obsessive interest and evaluate it not by realistic standards but by their own hopes. They spend hours listening to foreign radio stations, which come through with crackling and barely audible voices but still draw devoted audiences. News items, frequently misunderstood and even more frequently misinterpreted, are related to friends and circulate from mouth to mouth, becoming at each repetition more unreliable and fantastic. They may grow into obsessive ideas which fix a specific date when "Communism will collapse" or "the Americans will come." Reality at length refutes most of these rumors; nevertheless, while they live they are received by many, perhaps the more eagerly the more speculative they are.

The political forces that work at present in world affairs have raised up America as the most energetic opponent of Bolshevism. Anybody who wishes to see the end of the Red domination has to turn towards her as the natural ally, trusted friend, and long-awaited liberator. As an additional impetus, certain American institutions direct a regular flow of propaganda towards the satellite countries and speak of liberation in promising terms. The wistful people in the cold interpret these messages as the announcements of a political Hercules or an anti-Communist Davy Crockett. Instead of putting the statements into a realistic context they conjure up the image of a mythical hero—the American—who is capable of working wonders and is ready to defeat the might of Communism. This unrealistic and wishful image naturally evokes the disappointment that is so often caricatured in popular jokes. As one joke has it, the little fellow, having been expelled from the party, dreamed of President Eisenhower personally interceding on his behalf and asking the party boss to reinstate him in his membership. According to another joke, when the radio began to play a military march, an elderly lady hard of hearing delightedly explained: "Heavens above, the American army has arrived!"

It is a favorite function of modern psychology to explain the birth and life of myths. The American myth that exists in the satellite countries can be explained in rather simple terms. It is neither cosmogonal nor magical, but strictly political—it is the creation of those who feel defeated and search for a hero. In the rational world of politics, however, mythical ideas are dangerous. No political power can live up to superhuman expectations, none can promise, let alone work, miracles. The United States has a complex role on the stage of global politics and cannot play Davy Crockett. At crucial moments, such as the Hungarian revolution of 1956, she could not appear as a liberating Hercules and could not aid the freedom fighters by an omnipotent force of arms; as a result, the myth was shattered, and it was a myth that had been encouraged by herself. A propaganda that appeals to myth and promises the impossible is unrealistic and may fizzle out just when it is most needed.

Time and time again, the nonbeliever sees his hope of a miraculous change smashed. Together with hope, he loses his interest in the disappointing outer world. He withdraws into a shell, narrows his consciousness, and bars from his mind everything that is beyond sheer subsistence (this is the third type of reaction). Apathetically he drifts along in his daily routine. "In tyranny, everything is futile," said one poet, speaking with the voice of many.[4] Thus, Czarism produced a national character in Oblomov, and Communism brought about its own kind of drab apathy. It seems logical to assume that the rule of a monopolistic superego cuts down people's natural initiative, their courage to try innovations. Its impact is, naturally, more acutely felt in the satellite countries than in the Soviet Union. An informant from Hungary described his past as the time of "empty years and blank lives, when the days pass without happenings, the years without events; when there is nothing to look back on, nothing to recall as joyful, no memory worth remembering."

The mass apathy, like every mood, has its floods and ebbs that follow the cycles of party and police terror. A mounting wave of terror engenders greater apathy, while a political relaxation lures people out of their shells. The torpor, however, cannot be discarded, or reversed, at will; it leaves behind its psychological effects. After several cycles, lethargy becomes a part of the general attitude, a trait of the national character. The great old poet looked around and spoke: "This is a broken, tired, agonizing people."[5]

To be sure, this lethargy does not come from physical fatigue; it has nothing to do with muscular strain. The nonbeliever is tired of being commanded and oppressed. His apathy shows up in his relationship to his superiors, to the official mechanism of command and obedience. Those Hungarian refugees who after some years of an apathetic life reached the land of freedom were characterized by a sharp-eyed Western observer in these words: "They were accustomed to taking instructions, to complying with rules and regulations and to having decisions made by someone else. It was only when the element of choice entered into the picture that many of the refugees demonstrated their lack of capacity to make a decision for themselves. . . . Many preferred to be told, rather than decide for themselves."[6]

Unresolved strains that linger for a long time generally transform themselves into neurotic symptoms. It would be logical to expect that the regular operation of Communism would evoke neurosis, and more so in the satellite countries, where the regime is new, than in Soviet Russia itself, where time has permitted a greater degree of psychological accommodation. Indeed, many reports bear out this assumption.

A poet, musing before his desk, felt "nettled and tormented by demons." People of ordinary temperaments complain of nervousness and headaches and show symptoms of anxiety states, obsessions, and compulsive tendencies.[7] One informant, when entering his office, felt the imminent danger of being crushed by a heavy rock, and this fear of falling rocks, a well-known image in anxiety states, often pops up in the recollections of refugees. Obsessive ideas seize the sports fans, who take one soccer team, allegedly favored by the authorities, as the symbol of the regime. The team's defeat is an omen for the downfall of the regime and causes mass elation, while its victory puts thousands in a depressed mood. Compulsion is exhibited, for example, in small-scale, often senseless theft and sabotage. Such neuroses comprise the fourth reaction.

Whoever has to cope with heavy strains needs particular support and searches for it insistently. In America he may consult licensed healers and counselors and expect to receive ego support on the couch of the analyst, in the armchair of a social worker, or in the office of a marriage counselor. The comparable professions in the Soviet countries are under the control of the Red superego and offer help in proportion to the patient's faith. They do efficient work with believers and sincere compromisers, but many of the people in the cold are left to their own resources and have to restore their psychological balance through improvised self-cures. The utility of self-healing should not be underestimated and particularly not in the peasant societies of Europe. In the countries that are now ruled by Bolshevism, the old, hand-written cookbooks contain not only recipes for food but also formulas for folk medicine—for cold, stomach ache, or post-partum depression. However skeptical our age is on this point, the old formulas and self-invented cures work in practice amazingly well and do give psychological relief.

Among the self-administered remedies, religion is perhaps the most powerful in giving consolation and support. It satisfies important psychological needs at times when Communism fails, and it is able to withstand the pressures of the state power. Although the authorities suppress its institutional life, censor its announcements, and hamstring its activities, religion still survives in the daily practice of the people. Under the eyes of the official watchers, crowds fill the churches, participate in traditional rites, thumb worn-out prayer books, establish new sects, and even proselyte among the citizens.[8]

One refugee described with lucid insight that "inner hostility" that many in the satellite countries entertain towards the regime: "It is like a sorrow eating the soul away. One can forget it and then, again, one has to remember it. So it happened on that afternoon when, on my way home, a sudden sadness took hold of me. It was like the feeling of defeat. Still, I had to think of revenge and was seized by an impulse to set the world afire. Instead, I kicked our garden gate so hard that it broke off the hinges." A poet commemorated the same feeling: "Lo, how one's heart stills and turns trustful when, amidst eternal harrowing and harrying, he lives for a few hours by his own laws."[9]

This hostility, which is the fifth reaction of those in the cold, is seldom expressed or acted out but has to be repressed. It appears as a recurrent feeling, a passing mood which is otherwise dammed up by fear or channeled by the authorities against the permitted targets of aggression. It manifests itself in small-scale protest actions which do not go beyond the limits of safety. Theft, sabotage, carelessness, are just as common forms of protest as church attendance or other demonstrative identification with anybody or anything that dissents from the Red superego. A trivial example concerns a hardened criminal who broke out of the police jail and eluded a nation-wide dragnet; the law-abiding citizenry suddenly overlooked his crime and felt an emotional solidarity with him. Since he outwitted the hated police, the criminal became a popular hero, a political symbol.[10]

Minor protest actions are common, but few are the people who resist openly. Those who offer resistance must indeed have a rare inner strength, and they deserve our admiration. They are led by an individual superego so strongly opposed to the Red norms that it cannot compromise but has to assert its self. They have the courage to challenge the formidable power of the party state and to expose themselves to all the threatened punishments. They choose a tragic course which exacts heavy tolls and pays no reward. Their heroic deeds seldom earn public recognition but remain hidden in a police file.

Circumstances may drive all sorts of people into valiant resistance. In normal times, however, Communist administration operates smoothly and resistance seems futile, the party members toe the line obediently, and the people in the cold try to live peacefully. At such times it is those people who cannot find a place of their own in the existing social structure who are likely to put up open resistance; they have nothing to lose and see no incentive to go along with the regime. Among them are the adolescents who, passing through the storm-and-stress period of their lives and having no social responsibilities, turn out to be furious opponents of the system. To the frequent embarrassment of their parents, they establish an arsenal in the basement of the school, paste anti-Communist manifestoes on the walls, and fight with a ferocity unknown among adults.[11]

The neurotic—and psychotic—cannot find secure places either and have to suffer the plight that Bolshevism allots to social weaklings. Some official spokesmen contend that mental disorders originate in the iniquities of capitalistic exploitation and disappear in Communist society.[12] The contention is even more ridiculous than its counterpart that asserts that Communism puts an end to crime and prostitution. No factual evidence indicates that mental disorder is more common in capitalistic than in non-capitalistic society, and no theoretical reason exists why it should be so. What the official claim really means is that the party state does not tolerate mental disorders.

Intolerance or cruelty towards the neurotic and the psychotic is more common than is generally admitted. As a matter of fact, every society has its own rules of how to treat the usually troublesome neurotic and what place to assign him. He may receive veneration, tolerance, or ridicule just as well as punishment; and the treatment that Communist society gives him depends on the official policy. Stalinism, uncompromising as it was, did not show much philanthropy towards the emotionally disturbed individual but regarded him as a troublemaker or outright saboteur who must conform or be punished. Under the new policy of Khrushchev, a more tolerant attitude seems to have emerged which offers more help and applies more liberally the practices of Western psychotherapy, including psychoanalysis.[13]

The official guardians of norms and values have reasons of their own to dislike the mentally or emotionally unbalanced individuals. Neurotics and psychotics cannot be molded into ideal believers. On the contrary, by their very presence they disturb any Utopian plan. They are likely to be abnormally preoccupied with a superego and can dedicate to it all the attention and energy that the "normal" person would apply to the details of reality. They become emotionally involved when matter-of-fact actions are required, they exaggerate when reasonable submission is needed, they do not react to commands in the expected way. They may either approve or deny the prevailing superego of a society, doing so vehemently, aggressively, obsessively. They develop a fixation of ideas and emotions either around religion (as happens frequently in Anglo-Saxon societies) or around politics (common in the Soviet countries). The neurotic with a political fixation may turn against the Red regime with "abnormal" energy and openness. If his aggressive tendencies are overt, if his deprivation feelings are strong, then he may disregard the dangers, rational considerations, and all other conditions that keep the majority in line. He may end up in an institution of the terror agencies rather than in an institution of medical care.

One informant who claimed to have participated in a resistance group portrayed the leader in the following terms: "His booming voice immediately silenced everybody. He demanded unconditional discipline and kept a horsewhip in the drawer of his desk. He could have killed a person by whipping him to death." The truth of this portrait is irrelevant, since the wish is an integral part of every human expression. In this case, the desire for a horsewhip-brandishing leader, the juvenile admiration of a superman, and the unrealistic plan of the resistance organization constitute obvious symptoms.[14] The resistance movements, as they are compelled to operate under Communism, attract many neurotics and serve as the meeting places of two widely varying personality types, heroes and neurotics. Such an ill-fated association alone does much to doom opposition to failure.

The five types of reaction outlined above permit the people in the cold to carry on their lives—to reach accommodation, positive or negative, with the regime and to compromise with their consciences. Neither of the two masters can be easily satisfied. The regime is ever suspicious, on the watch. The conscience responds to the compromise with recurrent qualms or with a slowly gnawing sorrow. The qualms do not torment constantly, but increase and decrease with the turns of the political policies. A little success in private life or a relaxation in terror shifts the balance towards greater acquiescence, personal failure and growing oppression, towards resistance. People drift between the two moods like leaves in the wind, waiting for the rake of the gardener. The regime, wielding its political rake, controls the subjects without great difficulty.

II

The believer, the half-hearted follower, the opportunist, and "the man in the cold" represent the four basic attitudes that human beings can take towards a collective superego. Human attitudes, however, are changeable, ready to be molded under the influences of the outer world. People in the cold may become opportunists and even believers, and the opportunists may accept the faith or join those in the cold. Out of the many possible shifts, two are especially important in the dynamics of the Bolshevik movement: the conversion of the non-believer and the disillusionment of the faithful Communist.

Conversion is what the authorities desire. They aim to "activate the masses" and fill them with faith through propaganda and agitation. They boast of wonderful conversions—of a former princess, a Jesuit priest, or a conceited kulak turned into a devoted party member, a Stakhanovite, or a kolkhoz worker. Official statements should always be read with a critical mind, but there cannot be much doubt that the party receives its annual harvest of souls and increases regularly with new joiners. As a matter of fact, this is the essence of Soviet man-making. Every year the movement has to add some new believers and many sincere compromisers to those already in the fold. If it fails to do so, it cannot replace those who fall out, cannot maintain its vigor and power, and faces an inevitable end.

The second case, disillusionment with Communism, occurs more often than official statements admit. Its reasons may be as manifold as the reasons for joining the party. A motive that attracts people may just as well repel them. Those who join expect a satisfaction of their personal needs and evaluate the party by the actual gratification received. Man's wants, however, are difficult to satisfy. The party is a rigid organization, bent upon extending its belief and achieving its political aims. It satisfies those individual needs that can be directed into the channels of the official policy. If the individual is content with the channeled satisfaction, if his needs are plastic enough, he will serve the Red superego unswervingly; but if he does not tolerate channeling and wishes satisfaction on his own terms, wavering and backsliding must follow.

While the party is rigid, human character is changeable. Old age remodels the wants and pleasures of youth, and the creed that satisfied the young man may become disappointing with advancing age. An aching loneliness may be healed through subsequent marriage, and the fraternal services of the party may lose their appeal. One report pictured an upper-cadre man whose faith was shaken when he was jilted by his wife; another authentic although sentimental report recorded the backsliding of a Communist after the death of his beloved child.[15]

Deprivation suffered under Bolshevism alienates many but works in its own way, according to its own methods. The individual judges deprivation by subjective measures, by his expectations and preferences and by the achievement of his companions. Hence, the outcome is often surprising.

The Soviet man does not necessarily feel deprived although he lacks those cars, appliances, and other mechanical aids that the average American takes for granted. On the other hand, one good party member who gained promotion and success in just proportion to his abilities and desires suffered in the general housing shortage and could not obtain a "suitable" apartment. The partial deprivation was enough to alienate him from the party.

The planned economy, the role of the state as the sole employer, the scarcity of consumer goods, and many other features of Soviet life create occasions when the subject may feel deprived and dispossessed. It is both the strength and the weakness of every totalitarian system that it promises to satisfy all needs and sets itself up as the general guardian of all citizens. In this way it adds power to its might but must carry the blame for almost every fault. The citizen of a democratic country may be dissatisfied with his employer, his butcher, his local transportation company, and his TV station. He has four separate complaints against four independent entities, and he may hope that the faults will be remedied one by one. In Communism, the four similar complaints are directed against one central operator, the party state, which is bureaucratic in all its dealings, indifferent towards complaints, and rigid in offering remedies. It becomes the central source of many deprivations, and the greater power it wields, the more often it annoys and provokes. The feeling of deprivation, a dangerous possibility in Communist countries, was greatly enhanced by the brutal policy of Stalin, which shattered the illusions of many and moved some to escape from the country of unfulfilled desires.[16] At present, Khrushchev's policy aims to counteract this danger and makes many attempts to satisfy the citizens by an improved standard of living, greater tolerance, and a generally more flexible manipulation of the people.

Misplaced idealism is responsible for the disillusionment of intellectuals. To be sure, the intellectual, with his inquisitive mind, is always apt to explore all the available ideas and change his convictions repeatedly. He keenly analyzes his inner self and the outer world, articulately expresses his doubts, hesitates in matters of faith, and identifies himself ambiguously. Trotsky in his spiritual gyrations is a typical example. He served the revolutionary cause with a consistent, life-long devotion, but changed the principles of the cause now and then. Being a persistent intellectual inquirer, he could be equally at ease with Lenin as well as with such countertypes as the socialist Kautsky and the psychologist Alfred Adler. Believing in Freud and skeptical towards many of the totalitarian claims of Communist philosophy, he denied that a distinctively Marxist military doctrine, architecture, or veterinary science was possible.[17] His volatility and independence could not be fitted into the iron discipline of the party. He had to be ejected and, finally, destroyed. His fate was matched by many, some of them famed (such as philosopher and People's Commissar György Lukács) and others unknown beyond their small circle.

Whatever its origin is, disillusionment evolves slowly through a long and painful process. Those months and years that lie between the emergence of the first doubts and the ultimate break with the party are fraught with self-probing thought and indecision. The man who once had faith cannot lose it without a fight. One Communist was already shaken in his beliefs when the authorities jailed him; he was still hesitant when released two years later; and it took him another year before he made his final renunciation.

Like a winding road, disillusionment passes through three distinct phases. In the first phase, the believer comes to feel that the party does not satisfy his needs. Since he conceives his membership as being the result of objective causes, he cannot admit the subjective motives of his backsliding. He has to find an objective explanation; in other words, he has to project his dissatisfaction into the outer world. As the most obvious target, he puts the blame on the party and concludes that the party makes false promises, deceives, lies, and feigns. One may logically contend that the party deceives only those who want to be deceived; but there is no more logic in losing the faith than in turning into a believer. At any rate, the Communist backslider concludes that the party fails not in satisfying individual needs but in creating the ideal social and economic conditions, the promised earthly paradise. As one witness put it metaphorically, "Slowly I realized that the party promised me steaks, but gave stale bread instead." A poet expressed the same feeling thus: "We preserved our souls, but false gods shrewdly deceived our senses."[18]

In the second phase of the process, guilt feelings erupt and the person blames himself for perfidy. "I believe in human conscience," confessed a Communist writer, "and take my place on the defendant's stand." "Who will forgive me? Who will absolve me?" wailed an anxious poet. A less literate witness used a more vulgar style to express his self-abasement: "Like degenerate mongrels, we only moan, crouching forever, however great is the kick into our smarting flank."[19] In order to resolve his feelings of guilt, the disappointed individual re-examines Communism or approaches another superego. He is on the search without clearly realizing what he searches for; and his life and interests may turn in new, unexpected directions. He may make a conventional marriage, change his job, engage in the study of Stoic philosophy, or embrace the consolation of religion.

In the third phase, a final decision must be made to placate the conscience. Contrary to the popular opinion, the decision is, more often than not, to return to the party.

It must not be forgotten that faith is a changeable attitude, and one may at any time move from the state of doubt into the state of faith and back again. Many good Communists undergo crises of doubt; however, even the most tormenting doubts may be overcome by powerful motives tending to keep a person within the fold. For one thing, it is extremely difficult to leave the party at one's own will. The party, which ousts people so often, does not tolerate voluntary withdrawal. It tries to keep those it has selected and to strengthen the belief of those who waver.

Members who are discovered to be slipping away are often sent to special courses or put under the benevolent guidance of a trusted functionary. They receive a kind of common-sense group therapy, the same psychological treatment that the Alcoholics Anonymous in America uses for a different purpose. True, in many cases the faith cannot be completely restored.[20] However, relatively few doubters go so far as to make a final break with the party and embrace another creed publicly. This turn is more common in the Western countries, where Communists constitute a minority and the individual has the liberty to make his choice; but in the provinces under Soviet domination apostasy must be followed by an escape from the country, a bold and dangerous undertaking.

At any given time, many party members find themselves in one or another phase of disillusionment; however, few are those who complete the process, march to the end of the road, discard the Red philosophy, and confess their belief in another creed. These few are compelled to justify to themselves and to their friends their change of faith. Driven by conscience, they have to describe their experience with the superegos, to explain it reasonably and communicate it to others. A loss of faith usually precipitates a self-analysis, carried out not by means of scientific psychological terms but of those concepts which happen to be at the individual's disposal.

A complete self-analysis implies the unearthing of the nonconscious elements of the action, but this penetration is blocked by many circumstances. One's experience with a superego is never entirely conceptualized; its two fundamental elements, the appeal of the superego to certain psychological needs and the following ego-involvement, remain below the level of consciousness. In addition, the experience with one superego has to be expressed in the terms of another superego. The disillusioned Communist has to express his case in non-Communist concepts, norms, and values. Since every superego has its own terminology, the experience can seldom be translated with precision. When Earl Browder named "stupid policies" and "isolation" as the reasons why he had broken with the party, he hardly intimated what the mainsprings of his action really were.[21]

The very involvement of the ego is another block to clear expression. The loss of faith, like any other personal failure, is a complex and humiliating experience. When remembered, it is rationalized, styled, and fitted into an ideal pattern that can be approved by the self as well as by the outer world. Often it becomes stereotyped, since a stereotype benevolently veils individual shortcomings and adorns them with popular generalizations. Thus, the memory of apostasy and conversion omits personal needs and gratifications and tells a story of pleasing commonplaces—the story of the ingenue (or farmboy) caught in the sophisticated urban schemes of Communism, of the "pilgrim's progress" through the errors and sins of Communism towards the real Truth, of the erring girl whose fate was to meet an attractive seducer.

In view of such difficulties in communication, would not it be wiser to be silent? Alas, silence is not always a matter of wisdom, and speech in itself is often a natural remedy.

The trauma of a lost faith knows no better remedy than public confession. Converts and apostates have to speak, teach, and proselyte. The literates among them do even more—they "write out" what is on their mind. In the past, religious experiences were commemorated and world literature was thereby enriched with some masterpieces; in the present era of lively political concern, the experiences of the apostate from Communism are entrusted to writing. By now they make up a voluminous library of consummate works of art, best sellers, and pulp stories. They constitute a rich human documentary, a moving testimony, and valuable source material. They picture Communism in the form in which the apostates rationalize it after their apostasy. The true confessions that result from strong emotional impressions are not necessarily objective, frank, and penetrating accounts. Conscience is sensitive and timid and does not give away its secrets lightly. It is often more eloquent in silence than in words.

XI. MANIPULATION REASSESSED

THE REFUGEE WHO TOLD me the following story was a writer in Communist-dominated Hungary. Like many of his colleagues, he never joined the party. For each book and article he wrote he had to struggle hard with censors and editors. He could never express himself sincerely, and at every turn he had to compromise with the official instructions of the party. Still, he managed to live better than the masses by accepting the privileges which the regime deals out to creative intellectuals. Then, seizing an opportunity, he escaped from his native country and reached the freedom of the Western World. There he immediately set to work on an old, cherished plan: the writing of a sincere book about his experiences under Communism. But suddenly he realized that he could not write. He had the feeling that he had lost his ideas. His memories, his complaints, and his sufferings seemed to have become meaningless, and, when put into words, they appeared to be the thoughts of a stranger. Each sentence he put down sounded like a stranger's voice—as if somebody were whispering about him —and each sentence had to be erased. He struggled with himself for weeks and asked repeatedly: Was it the experience of Communism which inhibited in a free world the recording of the past? Or was it the experience of freedom which inhibited the recalling of the past? He could not answer, and he felt that he had lost his ability to write.

Our writer had served the regime as an opportunist, without devotion and with resentment. He thought that he was free from the influences of Communism and that by escaping he could obtain the full freedom to do as he liked. Yet, the story indicates that he was bound to the regime not by the force of command alone but also by personal involvement, and his involvement could not be shaken off easily. Having escaped from the power of the Red superego, he suddenly lost his creative ability, and this is a typical act of self-punishment. What was the guilt that remained unknown to him but demanded punishment and lamed his writing hand? Did he indict himself because of his complicity in Communist propaganda or because of his betrayal of the Communist masters? Apparently he felt guilty on both accounts and was haunted by a twofold infidelity. The stranger's voice in his thoughts whispered about his duplicity towards all his friends and ideals, and the ambiguity of his feelings crippled the real culprit, his writing hand.

I

Ambiguity of feelings towards a father or any powerful authority is a common element of human behavior, and it has a part in the relationship between man and Bolshevism. In this context the case of our writer makes two points. Because of this ambiguity, Communism influences more people than the citizens are willing to concede, and, for the same reason, it is extremely difficult to evaluate the results of the Communist manipulative techniques. Human reactions to Soviet man-making remain hardly known. It is impossible to draw up a balance sheet which would account for the various types of believers and non-believers, and all I can attempt is to answer the opening question of this study in a tentative way. My thesis is that it would be a gross self-deception to call Soviet man-making a failure.

At an early phase of its history, Communism drafted a plan for creating men of its own mold and developed methods to manipulate people to achieve the desired end. The methods were formulated through trial and error and changed repeatedly. Lenin, Trotsky, and the other fathers of the revolution had a romantic approach: they believed in an imminent world revolution and thought that all mankind could be reshaped in three glorious days. When the world revolution did not materialize, Stalinism shifted to a realistic, long-range program. It settled down to make men through a slow laborious process; and, with its rigorous insistence on all the demands of the Red superego, with its ample use of terror against any possible deviation, it settled for a process that was brutal, too. Then Khrushchev took the helm and (assuming that he represents a lasting policy and not a tactical change only) introduced a more flexible and tolerant way of handling human raw material.

The method developed primarily through practical experience, but one cannot entirely dismiss the idea that certain schools of psychology did affect its development. Stalin and his associates were familiar with the teachings of Pavlov and, if they ever thought in psychological terms, must have justified their policy with the concept of conditioned reflexes.[1] They used a stick as well as a carrot to condition the desired reflex and make the citizen respond to the official stimuli in the expected way. They worked crudely yet effectively; in fact, the same technique is widely used in the child-rearing practices of many countries.

At the same time, the Stalinist technique of manipulation had a weak point. It was rigid and mechanical and handled human material as does the refining operation that separates precious ore from useless slag. It clearly separated the citizens who responded correctly to the official stimulus from those who responded incorrectly; in other words, it divided the population into friends and enemies. Stalinism did not permit a third alternative, which may be obnoxious to logic but is always useful to psychology. Hence, it forced into the class of enemies many people whom a more flexible treatment could have turned into compromisers.

Khrushchev and his collaborators may or may not have studied the ideas of post-Freudian psychology, but, actually, no study was necessary. Since those ideas were popular in the West and well-known in the satellite countries, they might easily have found their way into the highest circles of Communist leadership. In any case, the new policy turned out to be more receptive towards Western ideas and relaxed the earlier censorship of modern psychology.[2] Concurrently, it abandoned the technique of conditioning one desired reflex, although it has not gone so far as formally permitting a third alternative. It applied sophisticated methods based on the observation that people have to "act out" and "talk out" their spontaneous reactions and that, having finished with that, they are ready to accept the suggestions of a psychotherapist or manipulator.

The 1961 program of the Communist Party of the U.S.S.R. gives some clues to the present manipulative technique, and its wording deserves our attention. The program calls for "educating a new man who will harmoniously combine spiritual wealth, moral purity, and a perfect physique," and describes the "moral code" of this man in such terms as "devotion to the Communist cause, love of the Socialist motherland, collectivism and comradely mutual assistance, human relations and mutual respect between individuals."[3] When this announcement is compared to the former manifestoes of the party, the changes in semantics appear to be slight. Yet, these changes intimate that the new technique of making Soviet men considers psychological needs and their satisfaction and endeavors to instill the Red superego accordingly. The new technique appeals to people's common desire for mutual assistance and respect; it tailors manipulation according to individual requirements, channels it towards people's needs, and allows one kind of treatment to the Poles and another to the Bulgarians.

With the methods that were available, Communism set out to form the first generation of Soviet men. Although it encountered unexpected resistance (perhaps that of the peasantry was the most stubborn), it nevertheless succeeded in reaching its basic goals. By 1945 believers and compromisers amounted to a sizable mass and lent stability to the regime. Part of this success must be attributed to the impact of World War II, to the rekindled nationalism in Russia, to the suffering inflicted by the invading Germans, and to the final victory on the battlefield. By the time the guns were silenced, the regime had established itself in the heart of the citizens and confidently made plans for a second Soviet generation.

As often happens with such vast planning, a mistake slipped into the calculations. Stalin applied to the satellite peoples the same, basically Russian formula that he had used before. He overlooked the diversity of cultures in the seven countries and underestimated the resistance of the seven peoples. With those peoples, the Russian formula did not seem to work, and the peoples did not submit. They escaped from Communism en masse, protested eloquently before the public opinion of Europe and America, and revolted with arms in their hands against the masters. They resisted Communism for many reasons; the most compelling reason, however, was that they were loath to become Soviet men and wanted to be themselves.

Resistance was strongest in the westernmost satellite countries which constitute a somewhat separate body within the Communist bloc and differ in essential features from the more acquiescent eastern societies. Czechoslovakia, Hungary, and Poland experienced three major historical changes—Reformation, Enlightenment, and Capitalism—which creatively formed Western mentality but hardly touched Russia. These changes introduced new norms and values and summoned the individual to make his choice among them. The monopolistic superego of the Middle Ages was defeated and could not support any longer the existing political and economic system. The holders of power lost their appearance of being superhuman guardians of norms, and the communal landholding of medieval serfdom gave way to private ownership. The well-articulated and eloquent individual superegos that emerged were pitched against one another and created a life of keen, general competition. Each individual was supposed to work for himself and forge his own success in political and economic life. Each government marched into power as the fortunate victor in competition and could not expect the protection of any power beyond that competition; each person managed his economic affairs so as to vie energetically for success and to amass money.[4]

It is the nature of competition that only a few can succeed, while many fail. Hence, competition in itself creates tensions and frustrations and lowers the threshold of frustration tolerance. People who live in a competitive society and are driven by strong individual superegos make a greater effort to pursue many goals, are emotionally attached to their goals, and expect happiness from reaching those goals. If any obstacle blocks their way, they react with direct aggression and try with all their strength to annihilate the causes of frustration. Their life is tense, alert, and anxious when compared to the easygoing unconcern of certain Oriental societies. "Their souls are mauled by unhappiness and private property," as a Communist poet with some malice remarked of them.[5] The words of the poet, however, express more than a slogan of the party; they express an old Oriental idea: the idea of non-competitive societies in which withdrawal and renunciation of the goal are the usual responses to setbacks.

Communism, when imposed upon a competitive, aggressive society, is a perennial cause of frustration and leads to revolt. The Poles, Hungarians, and Czechs did not experience a Czarist monopoly, did not believe in a Third Rome, did not sustain a general loyalty that could have been transferred to Communism. For them, life under Stalinism was a new and shocking experience, abhorrent in all its details. The policy of liquidating competition, of substituting collectivism for individualism, went against their most valued aims. In their eyes the issue was clear: Communism, like a Shylock, demanded a part of their dear self, their individuality. Hence, the masses in the cold reacted with direct attack.

These three relatively small countries are in sharp contrast with Russia, the great base of Communism. Russia has never experienced Protestantism, popular Enlightenment, and individual capitalism, anything that would have interrupted the continuous rule of the monopolistic superego. During all her history, her people became accustomed to accepting power and domination as a matter of faith beyond the control of the individual. They became accustomed to not criticizing the justice of the domination, to not raising unnecessary doubts, and to not making political decisions; they became used to a non-competitive economic life as well. Communal landholding, which survived in great parts of Russia up to the appearance of Communism, created an economy in which money was hardly used and the entrepreneurship of the individual was greatly restricted. Gogol expressed the popular belief when he depicted any striving for money as a knavish deal in dead souls. The Russian peasant was not supposed to compete, and when he did so, he pursued immaterial goals. He wanted more magic and religious grace, perhaps respectability and prestige, but not money.

Within a few weeks, the ancestral system of Czarism

gave way to Communism. From a psychological point of view the change did not represent a shocking experience. It required a transference of loyalty but no personal adjustment to a monopolistic superego. *Narodnost* (behavior becoming to the people) was the proper standard of conduct under Czarism, and *partiinost* (behavior becoming to the party), under Communism. The latter did not necessitate a redefinition of the individual's role in politics, competition, and personal advancement. Lenin's passionate rejection of the liberal idea of free competition fitted into the Russian tradition and contributed to the acceptance of his rule.

The public opinion of the West characterized the Russian with the stereotypes of "backward" and "collectivistic."[6] Let us not believe that all Russians are as much alike as eggs in a basket. However, a kernel of truth is often hidden in stereotypes, and the life of any group molds the characteristic behavior of the members. The Russian has an old heritage from medieval life: a tendency to repress his competitive desires and accept the frustration inflicted by political power and economic bondage. When meeting a setback, he renounces the goals of competition and shows a high frustration tolerance. He does not attack the collective superego, however frustrating it is, but rather expects his relief through it. This is why he seeks, again and again, to obtain mystical relief: through a holy man who can "hold your soul in his hand," through a revolutionary leader who is adored with a holy fear, or through any faith of whatever kind that requires dedication and sacrifice.[7]

Frustration, after all, is always subjective; the same experience may be frustrating for one man but not for another. A classical study in experimental psychology put five juvenile groups under "authoritarian" leadership, and while two of the groups responded with considerable frustration and aggression towards the leader, three groups reacted passively, with little or no frustration and no attempt to initiate group actions.[8] This observation, it seems to me, may be generalized. In tolerating frustration, great differences exist between men. The Western man gains satisfaction only when he is free to pursue his goals and assert his individual superego; the Eastern man regards this freedom as rather irrelevant. Accordingly, the Russians seem to be more willing than the Western peoples to accept what the Red domination has in store for them. They are less likely to refuse a collective superego, to ask for individual happiness and demand freedom of conscience. They experience less dissatisfaction and express it less promptly; they make a somewhat more stable adjustment to the existing regime. Their attitudes constitute the psychological basis for the plan of Communist man-making in general and for Stalinism in particular.

The first generation of Soviet men was formed with the aid of a manipulative technique that fitted the national culture of Russia but aroused open resistance in the satellite countries. Nothing is more terrifying for a totalitarian system than an open failure, and in this instance the failure came into public view at a critical time, the time that followed Stalin's death. The highest party leadership was engaged in one of its bitter fights over policy matters and personal power; however, it was willing to reappraise the situation and embark upon a new policy. Its decision stemmed not from fear but rather from the belief that the regime was strong enough to relax its severity and could obtain better results from leniency. Hence, the new policy aimed at decreasing the terror, raising the standard of living, and increasing the popularity of the system.

When their turn came, the local leaders in the satellite countries were just as much as their colleagues in Moscow divided into two factions, one of them supporting Stalinism and the other supporting the new policy. Finally, however, they refashioned their manipulative technique and, as a general rule, adopted a treatment which was more to the liking of their own peoples. The change of treatment, as happens in psychotherapy also, created some confusion in the minds of the citizens and caused some political embarrassment to the regime, well exemplified in the Polish unrest and the Hungarian revolution of 1956. Those spectacular explosions, however, did not change the course of events, and the new policy took roots within a short time.

At present the satellite leaders tend to speak of the "coming of age of a new generation" and of "our fight for realizing the program of human happiness," and the official press is glad to point out how much the citizens' attitude towards the regime has changed in the last few years.[9] Manipulation of people seems to be proceeding effectively. It has assuaged opposition, strengthened the popular support of the regime, and increased the number of halfhearted believers and compromisers. Communism is at work to print its indelible mark on the behavior of the satellite peoples, and the indications are that, unless the present trend is halted, the second generation of Soviet men may be produced within a time comparable to that required for the first generation.

Large-scale use of psychological manipulation is a matter of technique and organization, two requirements for success which are available to the Soviet men of power. Therefore, the Communist success in manipulating people must not be interpreted as moral or ideological superiority. This success does not prove that the Soviet system is better than others in solving the pressing problems of humanity, or that the Communist order is more sensitive in adjusting itself to people's needs, or that the Red superego is more appealing than any other political system. Any success is significant, to be sure, but success in one field should not be mistaken for an all-out achievement. Manipulative techniques can be used for any purpose and by any kind of people, and an unscrupulous manipulator may be more successful than an honest one.

The Communist success, on the other hand, does prove the might of the regime and the weakness of human nature. Man is highly vulnerable to manipulation, and our progress in knowledge and technology has not rendered him less susceptible but more so. His natural resistance is attacked and often overcome by the mass-communication media, by the sophisticated methods offered by psychology, and by the pressure of all-powerful modern organizations such as the totalitarian state. Facing such an onslaught, he is hardly able to maintain his personal autonomy and willingly or unwillingly succumbs to outside forces. The epoch of rugged individualists and lonely frontiersmen has passed; we are approaching the era of the manipulated man.

II

It is a modern idea of Western history (not much older than the Constitution of the United States) that every man has a right to pursue his happiness and neither state nor any other institution of society can obstruct this right. Faithful to this idea, Western man behaves as an autonomous agent, selects his norms and restricts the hold of collective superegos. He expects satisfaction by reaching self-set goals and, when blocked in his efforts, feels intense frustration. His idea, which welds happiness and freedom of conscience inseparably, has summoned generations of people to act, use reason, work hard, plan and strive, make revolutions and wars. It has produced its critics, too, who have repeatedly scored the "disintegrated" and "amorphous" way of life of the West. The critics, however, were not any more integrated and could never agree among themselves about the best creed that should replace this free individualism.

Communism is the modern idea of the Orient, recent but bound to its timeless place of birth. It shares the Oriental belief in the absolute necessity of a collective superego; but, inspired by Marxist philosophy, it preaches a centrally organized social justice and wants the state to dole out everybody's wealth, status, welfare, and happiness. The practical details of how social justice is centrally organized and entrusted to a bureaucratic machine are irrelevant in this respect. The scheme in itself denies individual happiness and freedom of conscience and demands a complete submission to a superego. It reduces the individual essence of personality and aims for a society of spirited ants and intelligent robots who work, build, fight, marry, and multiply, but in all their actions miss an essential human trait, the labors of conscience.

Ours is not the first epoch in history in which East has confronted West with such a fateful difference in the general outlook on life. Once Christianity faced Islam under similar conditions, engaged it in a furious fight of a thousand years without ever reaching the point of mutual understanding. Is it indeed a part of the human predicament that two superegos should never meet in harmony? As a matter of fact, some eternal barriers exist among them. Every superego creates its own means of communication, its own concepts and values, its own language and logic, and is unable to communicate accurately with any other superego. Democracy and Communism have persistently exchanged messages, and more profusely than once Christianity and Mohammedanism did, but they have failed to reach an understanding; even when they have used the same word, they have applied it in a different sense.

This lack of harmony spells danger and prompts the superegos to insulate themselves through closely guarded borders. In centuries past, each of them tried to live in a realm of its own, set up its well-secured political autarchy, and invoked the help of the natural defense given by space. They were able to establish long-lasting, stable realms because they were separated by distances hardly penetrated by man. China built up her Great Wall and Russia her censorship to stave off unwanted intrusions. In our era, however, man has overcome the obstacles of space, and his progress in technology has abolished geographical distances. The major creeds cannot count any longer on the protection given by political autarchy. Democracy and Communism are now close neighbors, divided by a low fence only, and their proximity enhances the dangers inherent in the situation.

The future is hidden, and the human mind is not permitted to pry out its secrets. It can, however, distinguish two paths leading towards the time to come. One is that of an open fight that lets force make the final decision, although the war between Democracy and Communism would in all probability show a greater fury than the knights of Charlemagne and the viziers of the Sultan ever knew. The other is the path of reason, which considers that the very proximity of two powerful organizations not only enhances the danger of each to the other but also facilitates understanding. The Great Walls of yore fell down, and our system of communication may enable us to realize the great wish of every superego—the conversion of the opponent. The possibility of transforming the other camp by peaceful means is present. It conjures up for Western man a Herculean task of great labors and great rewards, a task which he may ignore only at his peril.

NOTES

I. INTRODUCTION

1. For a list of the printed sources, see the Bibliography.

2. John Kosa, *Land of Choice: The Hungarians in Canada* (Toronto: University of Toronto Press, 1957), and "A Century of Hungarian Emigration," *American Slavic and East European Review,* 16 (1957), 501-14.

3. Alex Inkeles, *Public Opinion in Soviet Russia* (Cambridge, Mass.: Harvard University Press, 1950); and Jiri Kolaja, "A Sociological Note on the Anti-Communist Czechoslovak Refugee," *American Journal of Sociology,* 58 (1952), 289-91.

4. The frequency distributions were arranged in 2 by 2 tables, and the probability of association was tested by the Chi-square method. The significant associations were tabulated and inspected for possible clusters.

5. John Kosa, "Personality Characteristics and Attitudes Toward Communism: A Study of Hungarian Political Refugees," Paper presented at the 1962 meeting of the Canadian Political Science Association.

III. THE RED SUPEREGO

1. Joseph Stalin, *Notes of a Delegate and Class and Party* (London: Lawrence and Wishart, 1941), pp. 37-38.

2. V. I. Lenin, *Collected Works* (New York: International Publishers, 1929), IV, Book 1, 57.

3. David Shub, *Lenin* (Garden City, N.J.: Doubleday, 1948), p. 23.

4. Hitler, who identified himself with German racism, repressed his personal rebellion in a cruder, more primitive way in *Mein Kampf.*

5. A good collection of them can be found in Julian Towster, *Political Power in the U.S.S.R.* (New York: Oxford University Press, 1948), pp. 426-30.

6. *Party Life* (April, 1947), quoted by Frederick C. Barghoorn, *The Soviet Image of the United States* (New York: Harcourt, 1950), p. xv.

7. Nikolai Bukharin, *Historical Materialism* (London: Allen and Unwin, 1926), p. 67.

8. *Pravda,* July 12, 1957, reprinted in *Népszabadság,* July 18, 1957.

9. Bertolt Brecht, *Die Massnahme,* in *Gesammelte Werke* (London: Malik, 1938), II, 329-59.

10. *Szabad Nép,* November 10 and 11, 1953.

11. Mátyás Rákosi, *Szabad Nép,* June 13, 1948.

12. Speech reported in *New York Times,* February 19, 1956.

13. L. Németh, "Quelques Problèmes des Arts Plastiques dans la Période de Désagrégation du Capitalism," *Acta Historiae Artium Academiae Scientiarum Hungaricae* (Budapest: Hungarian Academy of Sciences, 1957), IV; József Herman, "Nyelvészet és valóság," *Nyelvtudományi Közlemények,* 1949; and

Ede Theiss, "Szocialista statisztika, polgári áltudomány," *Statisztikai Szemle,* 1953.

14. József Révai, *Társadalmi Szemle,* September, 1951; *Délmagyarország,* June 16, 1957; *Népszabadság,* August 13, 1957.

15. Concerning this slogan, see Maurice Thorez in *L'Humanité* (Paris), April 13, 1934, and *Győr-Sopronmegyei Hirlap,* October 16, 1955.

16. A. Rossi, *A Communist Party in Action* (New Haven: Yale University Press, 1949), p. 175.

17. Rossi, *A Communist Party,* p. 285; G. A. Tokaev, *Betrayal of an Ideal* (Bloomington, Ind.: Indiana University Press, 1955), pp. 124-25; and Alexander Barmine, *One Who Survived* (New York: Putnam, 1945), pp. 102 ff.

18. Rudolf Schlesinger, *The Family in the U.S.S.R.* (London: Routledge and Paul, 1949), pp. 248-49, 336.

19. *Szabad Nép,* May 19, 1950.

20. *Népszabadság,* June 30, 1957.

21. Speech of Khrushchev, *New York Times,* November 7, 1957.

22. *Magyar Szó,* London, May 17, 1957.

23. György Parragi's speech in the Parliament, *Magyar Szó,* May, 24, 1957.

24. *Népszabadság,* July 25, 1957; *Pártépités,* June 1, 1951.

25. *London Times,* August 27, 1957.

26. *Népszabadság,* April 21, 1957.

27. *Népszabadság,* July 5, 1957.

28. *Népszabadság,* July 6, 1957.

29. *New York Times,* November 7, 1957.

30. Ella Reeve Bloor, *We Are Many* (New York: International Publishers, 1940), p. 307.

31. Zoltán Vas, *Tizenhat év fegyházban* (Budapest: Szikra, 1945), pp. 6-7.

32. Arthur Koestler, *Darkness at Noon,* Chap. 12.

33. Whittaker Chambers, *Witness* (New York: Random House, 1952), p. 196.

34. Quoted in Merle Fainsod, *How Russia is Ruled* (Cambridge, Mass.: Harvard University Press, 1953), p. 144.

IV. WORK AND RITUAL

1. Marx and Engels, as quoted in V. I. Lenin, *Collected Works* (New York: International Publishers, 1929), XX, Book 1, 119.

2. Leon Trotsky, *The History of the Russian Revolution* (New York: Simon and Schuster, 1937), I, 149.

3. § 9 of Law 1949:20 tc. of Hungary.

4. Quoted in Harry Schwartz, *Russia's Soviet Economy* (New York: Prentice Hall, 1950), p. 137.

5. Julian Towster, *Political Power in the U.S.S.R.* (New York: Oxford University Press, 1948), p. 129.

6. Alexander Barmine, *One Who Survived* (New York: Putnam, 1945), pp. 109-11, 249-50, 285. As a well-known scene of Dostoevsky (*Brothers Karamazov,* Part I, Book 2) suggests, similar "public confessions" were popular customs in Orthodox Russia.

7. Nathan Leites and Elsa Bernaut, *Ritual of Liquidation* (Glencoe, Ill.: Free Press, 1954), pp. 73-77; and Alex Weissberg, *Conspiracy of Silence* (London: H. Hamilton, 1952), p. 288.

8. *Népakarat,* August 11, 1957; *Népszava,* July 9, 1961.

V. DEGREES OF PERFECTION

1. A. Rossi, *A Communist Party in Action* (New Haven: Yale University Press, 1949), p. 196.

2. Usage has changed the meaning of the word "cadre," which originally denoted the nucleus of the party, to denote the officials of the regime. See Stalin, *Mastering Bolshevism* (New York: Workers' Library Publishers, 1937), p. 36.

3. Quoted by Merle Fainsod, *How Russia is Ruled* (Cambridge, Mass.: Harvard University Press, 1953), p. 89.

4. Nikolai Bukharin, *Historical Materialism* (London: Allen and Unwin, 1926), p. 306.

5. Julian Towster, *Political Power in the U.S.S.R.* (New York: Oxford University Press, 1948), pp. 287-88.

6. Gabriel A. Almond, *The Appeals of Communism* (Princeton: Princeton University Press, 1954), pp. 177-78; and S. Diamond, "The Influence of Political Radicalism on Personality Development," *Archives of Psychology,* 29, No. 203 (1936).

7. Gyula Háy, "Miért nem szeretem," *Irodalmi Ujság,* October 6, 1956.

8. Isaac Deutscher, *The Prophet Armed: Trotsky* (New York: Oxford University Press, 1954), p. 447.

9. Mihály Farkas, *Szabad Nép,* October 11, 1954.

10. *Népszabadság,* August 4, 1957.

11. *Szabad Nép,* March 2, 1952.

12. *Népszabadság,* August 7, 1957.

13. § 126 of the Stalinist constitution of the U.S.S.R.

14. Tibor Déry, *Niki* (Budapest: Magvető, 1956).

15. *Népakarat,* August 9, 1957; *Magyar Szó,* May 10, 1957.

16. Alex Inkeles, "Social Stratification and Mobility in the Soviet Union," *American Sociological Review,* 15 (August, 1950), 465-79; James N. Ypsilantis and Samuel Baum, "Occupational Mobility of the Farm Population in Hungary," Paper presented at the meeting of the Rural Sociological Society, 1960; and John Kosa, "Hungarian Society in the Time of the Regency," *Journal of Central European Affairs,* 16 (October, 1956), 253-65. Recent studies published in Hungary use income and occupational groups as distinctive categories of socio-economic status. See, for example, Mrs. Aladár Mód, "Születésszám és életszinvonal," *Demográfia,* 1961.

17. *Report on Court Proceedings in the Case of the Anti-Soviet "Bloc of Rights and Trotskyites"* (Moscow: People's Commissariat of Justice of the U.S.S.R., 1938), p. 741.

18. *Report on Court Proceedings,* pp. 769, 737, 787.

19. Zoltán Zelk, "Nem illet engem," *Irodalmi Ujság,* May 5, 1956.

20. Y. M. Sokolov, *Russian Folklore* (New York: Macmillan, 1950), p. 638.

21. A. Rossi, *A Communist Party,* p. 196.

VI. CUSTOMS SUBDUED

1. Imre Varga, "A pörkölt," *Dunántul,* No. 16 (1956).

2. For example, the "County Days of Vas" featured 150 local meetings, exhibitions, performances, festivals, etc. See *Népszabadság,* May 17, 1958.

3. *Népszava,* July 11, 1961.

4. *Népszabadság,* August 2, 1957.

5. See the Decree of the Hungarian Council of Ministers 34/1953 M.T. on home-craft and applied folk-art industry; and *Népszabadság,* July 14, 1961.

6. Linda Dégh, *Kakasdi népmesék* (Budapest: Akadémia, 1955), Tale No. 4.

7. Y. M. Sokolov, *Russian Folklore* (New York: Macmillan, 1950), p. 618.

8. Imre Sarkadi, *Irodalmi Ujság,* March 13, 1954; Tamás Kő, *Népszava,* July 9, 1961.

VII. PROPAGANDA AS A MONOPOLY

1. V. I. Lenin, *Left-wing Communism: An Infantile Disorder,* in *The Essentials of Lenin* (London: Lawrence and Wishart, 1947), II, 596.

2. J. Stalin, *Report to the 17th Congress, 1934,* in *On Organization* (London: Lawrence and Wishart, 1942), p. 5.

3. Attila József, "Szociálisták."

4. *The London Times,* August 28, 1957.

5. Mátyás Rákosi, *A békéért és a szocializmus építéséért* (Budapest: Szikra, 1951), p. 48.

6. See *Népszabadság* and *Népakarat* between June 30 and July 13, 1957.

7. *Népszava,* July 11, 1961; *Népakarat* and *Népszabadság,* July 9, 1957; *Népszabadság,* July 12, 1957; *Népszabadság,* August 17, 1957.

8. *Népszabadság,* January 7, 1958.

VIII. THE TERROR OF THE PERFECT ONES

1. Hans Kohn (ed.), *The Mind of Modern Russia* (New Brunswick, N.J.: Rutgers University Press, 1955), p. 20.

2. For example, Joseph Stalin, *Dialectical and Historical Materialism* (London: Lawrence and Wishart, 1941), p. 31.

3. One has to remember that Sigmund Freud made a famous "analysis" of the last Czar, concluding that the Czar suffered from an obsessional neurosis which accounted for his being "overgood" and squeamish "like Koko in *The Mikado.*" See Ernest Jones, *The Life and Work of Sigmund Freud* (New York: Basic Books, 1953), I, 338.

4. Simon Wolin and Robert M. Slusser, *The Soviet Secret Police* (New York: Praeger, 1957), p. 194.

5. László Benjámin, "Legyetek éberek," *Uj Hang,* October, 1956; *Szabad Nép,* May 19, 1950; and *Népakarat,* July 11, 1957.

6. See, for example, the text quoted in *Ellenforradalmi erők a magyar októberi eseményekben,* Kiadja a Magyar Népköztársaság Minisztertanácsa Tajékoztatási Hivatala, "Fehér Könyv" (Budapest, 1957), IV, 102.

7. Lajos Tamási, "Rapszódia a józanságért és az igazságért," *Irodalmi Ujság,* August 11, 1956; and *Népszabadság,* July 11, 1957.

8. Stephen Gorove, "The New Polish Constitution," *Washington University Law Quarterly* (June, 1954), p. 263.

9. Aleksandr I. Tarasov-Rodionov, *Chocolate* (Garden City, N.J.: Doubleday, 1932), p. 180.

10. Mátyás Rákosi, *A békéért és a szocializmus építéséért* (Budapest: Szikra, 1951), p. 64; Lajos Szamel, *A szocialista törvényességről* (Budapest: Szikra, 1954); *Népakarat,* August 8 and July 17, 1957; *Népszabadság,* October 6, 1957; *Délmagyarország,* May 21, 1957; and Lajos Kónya, *Irodalmi Ujság,* October 20, 1956.

11. Gogol, "The Portrait"; Dostoevsky, "White Nights"; Avrahm Yarmolinsky, *Road to Revolution* (London: Cassell, 1957), p. 287; and Leopold H. Haimson, *The Russian Marxists* (Cambridge, Mass.: Harvard University Press, 1955), pp. 6, 32.

12. Ferenc Vajó, *Népszabadság,* July 24, 1957.

13. Pál Virágh, *Magyar Épitőmüvészet,* February, 1954.

14. Hungarian police code, Decree with the force of law 1955:22 tvr.; Tibor Pőcze, *Népszava,* September 23, 1956; and Ferenc Nezvál, *Népakarat,* July 11, 1957.

15. See the Goldenberg case in A. Yarmolinsky, *Road to Revolution,* p. 266; and Zoltán Vas, *Tizenhat év fegyházban* (Budapest: Szikra, 1945), p. 22 and *passim.*

16. Alex Weissberg, *Conspiracy of Silence* (London: Hamish Hamilton, 1952), pp. 175, 383; and Leslie Balogh Bain, "Cardinal Mindszenty Tells How He Was Tortured," *Look Magazine,* December 25, 1956.

17. Lajos Kónya and György Heltai, *Irodalmi Ujság,* October 20, 1956. See further Raymond A. Bauer and Edgar H. Schein (eds.), "Brainwashing," *Journal of Social Issues,* 13, No. 3 (1957).

18. Nikolai Bukharin, *Historical Materialism* (London: Allen and Unwin, 1926), p. 37.

19. *Népszabadság,* July 20, 1957.

20. Spelled out in the Hungarian penal code, Law 1950:2 tc., and the prison rule, Resolution of the Council of Ministers 1105/1954 mt. h.

21. A. David Redding, "Reliability of Estimates of Unfree Labor in the U.S.S.R.," *Journal of Political Economy,* 60 (August, 1952), 337-40.

22. László Benjámin, "Legyetek éberek," *Uj Hang,* October, 1956; *Népszabadság,* August 4, 1957; *Népakarat,* August 10, 1957; and *Szabad Nép,* October 18, 1954.

23. *Népszabadság,* August 11, 1957.

24. *Népszabadság,* January 29, 1958; *Népakarat,* August 8, 1957.

25. Anna Louise Strong, *The Soviets Expected It* (New York: Dial Press, 1941), p. 139; András Berkes, *Népszabadság,* July 10, 1957; and Isidor Schneider, *The Judas Time* (New York: Dial Press, 1946), p. 108.

26. József Csegei Nagy, "Bünhődés," *Alföld,* March-April, 1956; *Népszabadság,* January 23, 1958; and Konstantine Simonov, *Days and Nights* (New York: Simon and Schuster, 1945).

27. *Népakarat,* July 4 and 14, 1957; *Népszava,* July 9, 1961.

28. *Népszabadság,* July 13 and 15, 1961.

IX. THE BELIEVERS

1. Michael Cherniavsky, "Holy Russia," *American Historical Review,* 63 (April, 1958), 619, 621; Nicholas V. Riasanovsky, *Russia and the West in the Teaching of the Slavophiles* (Cambridge, Mass.: Harvard University Press, 1952), pp. 79, 121, 119; and Hans Kohn, *The Mind of Modern Russia* (New Brunswick, N.J.: Rutgers University Press, 1955), pp. 97, 63-64. Pogodin's ideas are repeatedly expressed in Tolstoy's *War and Peace,* for example, by Anna Pavlovna in the opening passage of the book.

2. Isaac Deutscher, *The Prophet Armed* (New York: Oxford University Press, 1954), p. 413.

3. *Népszabadság,* May 17, 1958.

4. *Népakarat,* July 28, 1957.

5. In this part of our study I greatly profited from two manuscripts written by Hungarian refugees. One manuscript, entitled "My Contemporaries," contained literary portraits of intellectuals; the other one, the autobiography of a clerical worker, described the party functionaries of a province.

6. Nicolas Berdyaev, *The Origin of Russian Communism* (London: G. Bles, 1948), p. 48; Gabriel A. Almond, *The Appeals of Communism* (Princeton: Princeton University Press, 1954), pp. 210-11; and Theodore Draper, *The Roots of American Communism* (New York: Viking Press, 1957), *passim.*

7. Irving Howe and Lewis Coser, *The American Communist Party* (Boston: Beacon Press, 1957), pp. 405, 444-45.

8. Lajos Tamási, "Most küzdöm végig," *Irodalmi Ujság,* August 20, 1955; Stewart Alsop, "Wanted: A Faith to Fight For," *Atlantic,* 167 (May, 1941), 594-97, and Leon Trotsky, *Stalin* (New York: Harper, 1941), p. 418.

9. G. A. Almond, *The Appeals of Communism,* pp. 104-5; and "Hatvan sevenaletta," *Népszabadság,* May 17, 1958.

10. Attila József, "Hét napja."

11. T. Draper, *The Roots of American Communism,* pp. 223-24; and I. Howe and L. Coser, *The American Communist Party,* pp. 249-61.

12. G. A. Almond, *The Appeals of Communism,* pp. 161-62; Max Bedacht, as quoted in I. Howe and L. Coser, *The American Communist Party,* p. 172; Mátyás Rákosi, *Szabad Nép,* November 7, 1951; and G. A. Tokaev, *Betrayal of an Ideal* (Bloomington, Ind.: Indiana University Press, 1955), p. 32.

13. John Strachey, *The Coming Struggle for Power* (New York: Modern Library, 1935), pp. 406-7.

14. Benjamin Gitlow, *The Whole of Their Lives* (New York: Scribner, 1948), pp. 100-2.

15. G. A. Almond, *The Appeals of Communism,* pp. 235 ff.

16. Leopold H. Haimson, *The Russian Marxists* (Cambridge, Mass.: Harvard University Press, 1955), pp. 97-103.

17. *Népszabadság,* July 10 and 12, 1957.

18. *Nők Lapja,* June 10, 1961.

19. Milovan Djilas, *The New Class* (New York: Praeger, 1957), pp. 39-40.

20. Mark G. Field, *Doctor and Patient in Soviet Russia* (Cambridge, Mass.: Harvard University Press, 1957), pp. 59-60; and Helmut R. Wagner, "The Cultural Sovietization of East Germany," *Social Research,* 24 (Winter, 1957), 414.

21. Gyula Pápay, *Népszabadság,* August 19, 1961.

X. PEOPLE IN THE COLD

1. Valentin Gonzalez and Julian Gorkin, *El Campesino* (New York: Putnam, 1952), pp. 10, 22.

2. Áron Tamási, *Irodalmi Ujság,* November 2, 1956.

3. Zoltán Zelk, "Visszhang," *Irodalmi Ujság,* July 7, 1956.

4. Gyula Illyés, *Irodalmi Ujság,* November 2, 1956.

5. Milán Füst, *Irodalmi Ujság,* November 2, 1956. For a similar opinion, see István Simon, *Irodalmi Ujság,* August 1, 1953.

6. *Citizen,* Department of Citizenship and Immigration, Ottawa (April, 1958),

p. 6. See further Audrey Wipper, "Response to Revolution Among Hungarian Canadians," *Berkeley Journal of Sociology,* 6 (Spring, 1961), pp. 73-95.

7. Lajos Tamási, "Rapszódia," *Irodalmi Ujság,* August 11, 1956; and *Népakarat,* July 26, 1957.

8. Ladislaus Rosdy, "Ungarn im Niemandsland," *Hochland,* 49 (1957); Pannonicus, "Ungarns Katholiken," *Wort und Wahrheit,* 8 (1955).

9. Lajos Kassák, "Bizodalom a szabadságban," *Irodalmi Ujság,* August 18, 1956.

10. Sándor Márai, *Napló* (Washington, D.C.: Occidental Press, 1958), pp. 43-44.

11. Vincent Savarius, "A gyermekek harca," *Irodalmi Ujság* (London), July 1, 1957; and Irwin T. Sanders, "Communist-dominated Education in Bulgaria," *American Slavic and East European Review,* 15 (1956), 373-75.

12. Joseph Wortis, *Soviet Psychiatry* (Baltimore: Williams and Wilkins, 1950), pp. 86 ff.

13. György Vukovich, "Az alkoholizmus egyes demográfiai és szociális jellemzői," *Demográfia,* 1961; and Mihály Bálint, *Az orvos, a betege és a betegség* (Budapest Akadémia, 1961).

14. The same symptoms can be repeatedly met in the hero worship of the Russian revolutionary movements in Czarist times.

15. G. A. Tokaev, *Betrayal of an Ideal* (Bloomington, Ind.: Indiana University Press, 1949), p. 71.

16. Richard M. Stephenson and Jay Schulman, "Some Latent Sources of Economic Deprivation Among Non-Communist Hungarian Refugees," Paper presented at the meeting of the Eastern Sociological Society, 1958.

17. Isaac Deutscher, *The Prophet Armed* (New York: Oxford University Press, 1954), pp. 35, 70, 182, 193, 482.

18. László Benjámin, "Töredék," *Irodalmi Ujság,* July 28, 1956.

19. Tibor Déry, *Irodalmi Ujság,* November 2, 1956; Lajos Kónya, *Irodalmi Ujság,* August 11, 1956; *Szeged Népe,* November 4, 1956.

20. Such cases frequently occurred among cadre people. See Mátyás Rákosi, *A békéért és a szocializmus építéséért* (Budapest: Szikra, 1951), p. 78.

21. *The Louisville Courier-Journal,* October 18, 1954.

XI. MANIPULATION REASSESSED

1. See Sergei Chakhotin, *The Rape of the Masses* (New York: Alliance, 1940).

2. Concerning the permission of psychoanalysis and "psychic phenomena," see Mihály Bálint, *Az orvos, a betege és a betegség* (Budapest: Akadémia. 1961); and Milan Ryzl, "Research on Telepathy in Soviet Russia," *Journal of Parapsychology,* 25 (1961).

3. *New York Times,* August 1, 1961. For an interesting comment from Russia, see *New York Times,* October 8, 1961; from Hungary, *Népszabadság,* August 23, 1961.

4. David Mitrany, *Marx Against the Peasant* (Chapel Hill: University of North Carolina Press, 1951); John Kosa, "The Early Period of Anglo-Hungarian Contact," *American Slavic and East European Review,* 13 (1954), and "Hungarian Society in the Time of the Regency," *Journal of Central European Affairs,* 16 (1956).

5. Péter Kuczka, *Irodalmi Ujság,* November 7, 1953.

6. William Buchanan and Hadley Cantril, *How Nations See Each Other* (Urbana, Ill.: University of Illinois Press, 1953; and John Kosa, "The Rank Order of Peoples," *Journal of Social Psychology,* 46 (1957).

7. Dostoevsky, *Brothers Karamazov,* Part I, Book 2; Leopold H. Haimson, *The Russian Marxists* (Cambridge, Mass.: Harvard University Press, 1955), p. 6; and Nicolas Berdyaev, *The Origin of Russian Communism* (London: G. Bles, 1948), p. 9.

8. Kurt Lewin, Ronald Lippit, and Ralph K. White, "Patterns of Aggressive Behavior in Experimentally Created Social Climates," *Journal of Social Psychology,* 10 (1939).

9. Jenő Fock, *Hétfői Hirek,* August 21, 1961; György Marosán, *Népszabadság,* August 20, 1961; and Ferenc Sárdi, *Szabad Föld,* August 20, 1961.

BIBLIOGRAPHY

IN ENGLISH

Books and Articles

Almond, Gabriel A. *The Appeals of Communism.* Princeton: Princeton University Press, 1954.

Alsop, Stewart. "Wanted: A Faith to Fight For," *Atlantic,* 167 (May, 1941), 594-97.

Bain, Leslie Balogh. "Cardinal Mindszenty Tells How He Was Tortured," *Look Magazine,* 20 (December 25, 1956), 21-25.

Barghoorn, Frederick C. *The Soviet Image of the United States.* New York: Harcourt, 1950.

Barmine, Alexander. *One Who Survived.* New York: Putnam, 1945.

Bauer, Raymond A., and Schein, Edgar H. (eds.). "Brainwashing," *Journal of Social Issues,* 13, No. 3 (1957).

Berdyaev, Nicolas. *The Origin of Russian Communism.* London: G. Bles, 1948.

Bloor, Ella Reeve. *We Are Many.* New York: International Publishers, 1940.

Buchanan, William and Cantril, Hadley. *How Nations See Each Other.* Urbana, Ill.: University of Illinois Press, 1953.

Bukharin, Nikolai. *Historical Materialism.* London: Allen and Unwin, 1926.

Chakhotin, Sergei. *The Rape of the Masses.* New York: Alliance, 1940.

Chambers, Whittaker. *Witness.* New York: Random House, 1952.

Cherniavsky, Michael. "Holy Russia: A Study in the History of an Idea," *American Historical Review,* 63 (April, 1958), 617-37.

Deutscher, Isaac. *The Prophet Armed: Trotsky.* New York: Oxford University Press, 1954.

Diamond, S. "The Influence of Political Radicalism on Personality Development," *Archives of Psychology,* 29, No. 203 (1936), 53.

Djilas, Milovan. *The New Class.* New York: Praeger, 1957.

Dostoevsky, F. M. *The Brothers Karamazov.* Translated by Constance Garnett. New York: Macmillan, 1951.

———. *White Nights and Other Stories.* Translated by Constance Garnett. London: Heinemann, 1923.

Draper, Theodore. *The Roots of American Communism.* New York: Viking Press, 1957.

Fainsod, Merle. *How Russia is Ruled.* Cambridge, Mass.: Harvard University Press, 1953.

Field, Mark G. *Doctor and Patient in Soviet Russia.* Cambridge, Mass.: Harvard University Press, 1957.

Gitlow, Benjamin. *The Whole of Their Lives.* New York: Scribner, 1948.

Gogol, N. V. *The Overcoat and Other Stories.* Translated by Constance Garnett. New York: Knopf, 1923.

Gonzalez, Valentin and Gorkin, Julian. *El Campesino.* New York: Putnam, 1952.

Gorove, Stephen. "The New Polish Constitution," *Washington University Law Quarterly* (June, 1954), 261-82.

Haimson, Leopold H. *The Russian Marxists.* Cambridge: Harvard University Press, 1955.

Howe, Irving, and Coser, Lewis. *The American Communist Party.* Boston: Beacon Press, 1957.

Inkeles, Alex. *Public Opinion in Soviet Russia.* Cambridge, Mass.: Harvard University Press, 1950.

———. "Social Stratification and Mobility in the Soviet Union," *American Sociological Review,* 15 (August, 1950), 465-79.

Koestler, Arthur. *Darkness at Noon.* New York: Macmillan, 1955.

Kohn, Hans. *The Mind of Modern Russia.* New Brunswick, N.J.: Rutgers University Press, 1955.

Kolaja, Jiri. "A Sociological Note on the Anti-Communist Czechoslovak Refugee," *American Journal of Sociology,* 58 (November, 1952), 289-91.

Kosa, John. "Hungarian Society in the Time of the Regency,"

Journal of Central European Affairs, 16 (October, 1956), 253-65.

——. *Land of Choice: The Hungarians in Canada.* Toronto: University of Toronto Press, 1957.

——. "The Rank Order of Peoples," *Journal of Social Psychology,* 46 (November, 1957), 311-20.

Leites, Nathan, and Bernaut, Elsa. *Ritual of Liquidation.* Glencoe, Ill.: Free Press, 1954.

Lenin, V. I. *Collected Works.* Vols. IV-XXI. New York: International Publishers, 1927-29.

——. *The Essentials of Lenin.* London: Lawrence and Wishart, 1947.

Mitrany, David. *Marx Against the Peasant.* Chapel Hill: University of North Carolina Press, 1951.

Redding, A. David. "Reliability of Estimates of Unfree Labor in the U.S.S.R.," *Journal of Political Economy,* 60 (August, 1952), 337-40.

Report on Court Proceedings in the Case of the Anti-Soviet "Bloc of Rights and Trotskyites." Moscow: People's Commissariat of Justice of the U.S.S.R., 1938.

Riasanovsky, Nicholas V. *Russia and the West in the Teaching of the Slavophiles.* Cambridge, Mass.: Harvard University Press, 1952.

Rossi, A. *A Communist Party in Action.* New Haven: Yale University Press, 1949.

Ryzl, Milan. "Research on Telepathy in Soviet Russia," *Journal of Parapsychology,* 25 (June, 1961), 75-85.

Sanders, Irwin T. "Communist-dominated Education in Bulgaria," *American Slavic and East European Review,* 15 (October, 1956), 364-81.

Schlesinger, Rudolf. *The Family in the U.S.S.R.* London: Routledge and Paul, 1949.

Schneider, Isidor. *The Judas Time.* New York: Dial Press, 1946.

Schwartz, Harry. *Russia's Soviet Economy.* New York: Prentice Hall, 1950.

Shub, David. *Lenin.* Garden City, N.J.: Doubleday, 1948.

Simonov, Konstantine. *Days and Nights.* New York: Simon and Schuster, 1945.

Sokolov, Y. M. *Russian Folklore.* New York: Macmillan, 1950.

Stalin, Joseph. *Dialectical and Historical Materialism.* London: Lawrence and Wishart, 1941.

———. *Mastering Bolshevism.* New York: Workers' Library Publishers, 1937.

———. *Notes of a Delegate and Class and Party.* London: Lawrence and Wishart, 1941.

———. *Report to the 17th Congress, 1934,* in *On Organization.* London: Lawrence and Wishart, 1942.

Strachey, John. *The Coming Struggle for Power.* New York: Modern Library, 1935.

Strong, Anna Louise. *The Soviets Expected It.* New York: Dial Press, 1941.

Tarasov-Rodionov, Aleksandr I. *Chocolate.* Garden City, N.J.: Doubleday, 1932.

Tokaev, G. A. *Betrayal of an Ideal.* Bloomington, Ind.: Indiana University Press, 1955.

Tolstoy, L. N. *War and Peace.* Translated by Louise and Aylmer Maude. New York: Oxford University Press, 1957.

Towster, Julian *Political Power in the U.S.S.R.* New York: Oxford University Press, 1948.

Trotsky, Leon. *The History of the Russian Revolution.* New York: Simon and Schuster, 1937.

———. *Stalin.* New York: Harper, 1941.

Wagner, Helmut R. "The Cultural Sovietization of East Germany," *Social Research,* 24 (Winter, 1957), 395-426.

Weissberg, Alex. *Conspiracy of Silence.* London: Hamish Hamilton, 1952.

Wipper, Audrey. "Response to Revolution Among Hungarian Canadians," *Berkeley Journal of Sociology,* 6 (Spring, 1961), 73-95.

Wolin, Simon, and Slusser, Robert M. *The Soviet Secret Police.* New York: Praeger, 1957.

Wortis, Joseph. *Soviet Psychiatry.* Baltimore: Williams and Wilkins, 1950.

Yarmolinsky, Avrahm. *Road to Revolution.* London: Cassell, 1957.

Newspapers

Citizen, Department of Citizenship and Immigration, Ottawa (1958).

The London Times (1957).

The Louisville Courier-Journal (1954).

The New York Times (1956-61).

Unpublished Material

Kosa, John. "Personality Characteristics and Attitudes Toward Communism: A Study of Hungarian Political Refugees," Paper presented at the meeting of the Canadian Political Science Association, 1962.

Stephenson, Richard M., and Schulman, Jay. "Some Latent Sources of Economic Deprivation Among Non-Communist Hungarian Refugees," Paper presented at the meeting of the Eastern Sociological Society, 1958.

Ypsilantis, James N., and Baum, Samuel. "Occupational Mobility of the Farm Population in Hungary," Paper presented at the meeting of the Rural Sociological Society, 1960.

IN HUNGARIAN

Book and Articles

Bálint, Mihály. *Az orvos, a betege és a betegség.* Budapest: Akadémia, 1961.

Dégh, Linda. *Kakasdi népmesék.* Budapest: Akadémia, 1955.

Déry, Tibor. *Niki.* Budapest: Magvető, 1956.

Ellenforradalmi erők a magyar októberi eseményekben. "Fehér Könyv." Vols. I-IV. Budapest: A Magyar Népköztársaság Minisztertanácsa Tájékoztatási Hivatala, 1957.

Herczeg, István. "A kártéritési felelősség szocialista alapjai," *Jogtudományi Közlöny,* 1954.

Herman, József. "Nyelvészet és valóság," *Nyelvtudományi Közlemények,* 1949.

József, Attila. *Összes müvei.* Vols. I-III. Budapest: Akadémia, 1952-58.

Lukács, György. Irástudók felelőssége. Moszkva: Idegennyelvü Kiadó, 1944.

Magyar Statisztikai Zsebkönyv. Vol. XVI. Budapest: Központi Statisztikai Hivatal, 1956.

Mód, Mrs. Aladár. "Születésszám és életszinvonal," *Demográfia*, 1961.

Márai, Sándor. *Napló*. Washington, D.C.: Occidental Press, 1958.

Nagy, József Csegei. "Bünhődés," *Alföld*, 1956.

Rákosi, Mátyás. *A békéért és a szocializmus építéséért*. Budapest: Szikra, 1951.

Szamel, Lajos. *A szocialista törvényességről*. Budapest: Szikra, 1954.

Theiss, Ede. "Szocialista statisztika, polgári áltudomány," *Statisztikai Szemle*, 1953.

Varga, Imre. "A pörkölt," *Dunántul*, 1956.

Vas, Zoltán. *Tizenhat év fegyházban*. Budapest: Szikra, 1945.

Vukovich, György. "Az alkoholizmus egyes demográfiai és szociális jellemzői," *Demográfia*, 1961.

Newspapers

Délmagyarország (1957)

Győr Sopronmegyei Hirlap (1955)

Hétfői Hirek (1961)

Irodalmi Ujság (Budapest) (1953-56)

Irodalmi Ujság (London) (1957)

Magyar Épitőmüvészet (1954)

Magyar Közlöny. Hivatalos Lap (1949-54)

Magyar Szó (London) (1957)

Népakarat (1957-58)

Népszabadság (1957-61)

Népszava (1956, 1961)

Nők Lapja (1961)

Pártépités (1951)

Szabad Föld (1961)

Szabad Nép (1948-56)

Szeged Népe (1956)

Társadalmi Szemle (1951-54)
Uj Hang (1956)

Unpublished Material

"Autobiographical Notes" (manuscript furnished by a Hungarian refugee).
"My Contemporaries" (manuscript furnished by a Hungarian refugee).

IN OTHER LANGUAGES

Brecht, Bertolt. *Gesammelte Werke.* Vols. I-II. London: Malik, 1938.
L'Humanité (Paris) (1934).
Németh, L. "Quelques problèmes des arts plastiques dans la période de désagrégation du capitalism." *Acta Historiae Artium Academiae Scientiarum Hungaricae.* Budapest: Hungarian Academy of Sciences, 1957.
Pannonicus. "Ungarns Katholiken," *Wort und Wahrheit,* 1955.
Rosdy, Ladislaus. "Ungarn im Niemandsland," *Hochland,* 1957.

INDEX